LANCAST SQUADRONS

OF WORLD WAR II

IN FOCUS

SPECIAL EDITION

RED
KITE

First Published in 2002
This revised and expanded edition published in 2012 by,

Red Kite
PO Box 223
Walton on Thames
Surrey
KT12 3YQ
Tel. 0845 095 0346

www.redkitebooks.co.uk
www.wingleader.co.uk

Profile art by Piotr Forkasiewicz.
contact email: piotr_forkasiewicz@wp.pl

Printed in Poland by Dimograf Sp. zo.o.

ISBN 978-1-906592-05-9

LANCASTER SQUADRONS

OF WORLD WAR II

IN FOCUS

by
MARK POSTLETHWAITE

RED KITE

ACKNOWLEDGEMENTS

The task of finding photographs to illustrate over 60 different Lancaster squadrons can best be described as a bit of a challenge! However, with the help of many friends, authors and, most importantly, the Lancaster veterans themselves, we have managed to put together what you see in front of you. Many photographs in this album have passed through various people before arriving with us so we apologise if the name of the original photographer of any photo is not listed below. Also special thanks to Alex Bateman for providing answers to some of the really difficult questions!

PHOTOGRAPHIC CONTRIBUTORS

Simon Parry
Chaz Bowyer
Ron Mackay
Roy Nesbit
Andy Thomas
Dennis Clack
Chris Goss
Elizabeth Ellis
Aneurin Owen
E R Tanner
Alistair Lamb
George Wood
Peter Norton
Ron Newbery
C J Wyatt
Joyce Philo
George Knott
Ron Rodgers
Roger E Wallis
Margery Griffiths
Joe Hartshorn
R K Hardy
Ted Groom
John Banks
Jack Warwick
HC Hernamen
Ian Le Sueur
J Nicholas
Dennis Nolan
Joyce Dolling
Tommy Bishop
Paddy Tilson
Nigel Parker
ww2images.com

For Szymek my son, in the hope that he and his friends will never be called upon to show the courage and bravery displayed by the men of RAF Bomber Command.
MP

CONTENTS

INTRODUCTION

The problem for any author putting together a book on the Avro Lancaster is knowing where to draw the line. A classic aircraft such as the Lancaster was used by so many different units and airforces and in so many roles that to cover them all invariably means that one is left with a fairly bland overview. As this series of books is based on World War II types, we decided to limit the scope of this book to squadrons that flew at least one operational sortie during the war.

Over 60 squadrons flew the Avro Lancaster operationally during World War Two. Whilst some were old established units operating from well equipped pre-war airfields, the majority were formed within the rapid expansion of RAF Bomber Command in 1943/1944 and operated from the equally hastily created airfields that were carved out of the bleak Lincolnshire landscape.

Each squadron was different, some were lucky, others were not. Some were always in the limelight, others barely got a mention. Often there was great rivalry between units, especially when based on the same airfield, but when in the air they were as one and equal danger was faced by all.

This is borne out by the statistics which show that, generally, squadron losses were in direct proportion to the number of sorties flown. The only variable to this equation is the period in which the Lancaster was operated. If the squadron flew her through the traumatic winter of 1943, when Bomber Command was suffering appalling losses over Berlin then its casualty rate would be higher than that of a unit formed in the closing months of the war when Allied air superiority allowed the bombers to roam far and wide in daylight.

Aside from this then, the general parity between losses is simply a reflection of the randomness in which death chose the Bomber Boys. Flak made no distinction between rank or experience. An experienced crew could shake off a fighter, if they saw it, but a well aimed flak burst could not be countered. Every man in every bomber knew this. They knew that as soon as they took off on an operational sortie, their survival was realistically out of their hands. They also knew in the dark days of 1943 that the odds of them surviving a full tour of ops, which they had to complete, were less than 1 in 6.

The fact that these young men accepted these odds and took their Lancasters to war night after night is almost beyond our modern day comprehension. They were heroes in the truest sense of the word and this book is respectfully dedicated to every one of them.

SPECIAL EDITION UPDATE

When we published the first 'Lancaster Squadrons in Focus' back in 2002 it proved to be an immediate success and sold out very quickly. The obvious thing to do was reprint it but, having collected many new Lancaster photos in the following years, we decided that it would be better to try to aim for a 'Special Edition' rather than a straight reprint. As such, we've added an extra 32 pages, produced a brand new set of colour profiles by the amazingly talented Piotr Forkasiewicz, and wherever possible, replaced the old photographs with over 200 new ones. Of course, some squadrons were rarely photographed so we've had to use the same ones as before, however in most cases we've enlarged and enhanced them to provide a far better reproduction in this new version. It has also been possible to identify some previously unknown aircraft in the old photos so again we've kept those in with the new information.

Lancaster R5669 OL-E lies in a slightly worse state than that in which she set out in late 1942. Squadron Leader Roy Elliott, christened this Lancaster 'HMT River Spey', in tribute to the trawler that rescued him and his crew when his Wellington ditched in 1941.

THE AVRO LANCASTER

SPECIFICATION (BMkI)

Length
69ft 6 inches

Height
20ft 4 inches

Wingspan
102ft

Engines
Four x 1640hp Rolls-Royce Merlin XX, 22 or 24

Crew
7

Max Speed
275mph

Cruising Speed
200mph at 15,000ft

Service Ceiling
19,000ft

Maximum Range
2530 miles with 7000lb bomb load

Maximum Bomb Load
22,000lb

Defensive Armament
8 x .303 Machine guns two in nose and mid upper turrets, four in tail turret

Above: The prototype Lancaster BT308 made her first flight on 9th January 1941. It was realised fairly early on that the small triple Manchester fin arrangement was insufficient to handle the effect of the four powerful Merlins, so two larger fins were installed within a few weeks.
Below: Photographed some years later, BT308 not only has her new fins but also a jet engine installed! (This was an experimental Metrovick F2/1 turbojet fitted whilst she was on loan to Armstrong-Whitworth).

Above: The second prototype Lancaster DG595 photographed on 22nd August 1941 whilst being evaluated by the A&AEE. It is a testament to the soundness of the original design that this aircraft is visually almost identical to the last of the 7377 Lancasters built, unlike for example the Spitfire or Halifax.

The genius of the basic Lancaster design is demonstrated by how little it was modified throughout its production life. The specifications laid out above for the BMkI more or less relate to all of the 7377 examples that were built.

The only significant differences to this framework were as follows:
MkII Fitted with Hercules VI or Hercules XVI radial engines.
MkIII Fitted with American built Packard Merlin 28, 38 or 224 engines.
MkVI Fitted with more powerful Merlin 85 or 87 engines.
MkVII Fitted with a repositioned electrically operated Martin mid-upper turret and an FN82 rear turret, both with twin .5 calibre Browning machine guns.
MkX No visual difference to MkIII, simply licence built in Canada although the later examples were fitted with the Martin mid-upper turret.

All individual aircraft could be modified in the field with new or alternative equipment. This meant that even early production models could be seen with late war modifications, (if they lasted that long). This is nicely illustrated by the photo of W4154 on page 125, a very early MkI with a late war Rose rear turret. Indeed some airframes even managed to change Marks, coming off the production line as MkIs but later being fitted with Packard Merlins making them, in theory, MkIIIs. The identification therefore of a Lancaster by its Mark is of little practical use and is not generally referred to in this book.

EARLY PRODUCTION MODELS

The most identifiable feature of the very early Lancasters was the 'Special Night' black paint applied to the undersurfaces and fuselage sides. It had been designed to be an 'extra matt' finish but in practice it became patchy very quickly leading to a very scruffy appearance. In 1942 it was decided to revert back to the original 'Night' paint which had a smoother and slightly glossier appearance. The Lancaster pictured above, L7540 OL-U was 17th off the production line and shows the patchy finish well. Also visible are the early 'needle blade' propellers. These were standard on all Lancasters until more powerful Merlin engines were introduced and a broader 'paddle blade' prop was used. Generally, the paddle bladed propeller started to appear around mid-1944.

This Lancaster 'The Endeavour' shows many features of an early Lancaster such as:

1) Shallow bomb aimer's blister.

2) Pitot tube under the bomb aimer's window.

3) Observation blister on port side of the cockpit (often deleted on later examples, the starboard blister was usually retained).

4) The scruffy 'Special Night' finish to the undersides.

5) Smaller rectangular window below and behind the bomb aimer's blister.

6) Light coloured framework in the nose turret. Early Lancasters featured this in both the nose and tail turrets.

7) The light coloured stripe is tape stuck over the transport joint. This was a place where the Lancaster fuselage could easily be dismantled into sections.

8) This attachment point with a wire running up to the aerial was for the TR9 radio which was removed from around mid-1943.

LATE PRODUCTION MODELS

Throughout its wartime service, the Lancaster visually changed very little. However there were several important modifications which can help date when a photograph was taken. The above photo shows a standard late-war Lancaster fresh off the production line. Note the Rebecca aerials behind the nose turret, the paddle bladed propellers and the smoother 'Night' black finish to the fuselage sides.

Below: This Lancaster of 153 Squadron photographed in 1945 shows many features associated with later Lancasters such as:

1) Large bomb aimer's blister, introduced from early 1943.

2) Repositioned and reshaped oval window beneath and behind blister first seen in 1944. (see page 17)

2a) Sometimes this window had a perspex blister positioned over it to allow the bomb-aimer to see behind and below.

3) Repositioned pitot tube from 1944.

4) 'Z' equipment rings (see panel above).

5) Rebecca aerial used for blind approaches which replaced the earlier 'Lorenz' 'towel rail' aerial situated below the rear fuselage*. Rebecca was introduced in mid-1944. *see page 13.

6) Dark painted framework inside the nose turret seen from late 1942.

7) Semi-matt smooth black painted undersides introduced in 1942.

Interestingly, this aircraft retains the port-side cockpit blister.

'Z' EQUIPMENT AND 'VILLAGE INN'

A very common and distinctive feature on many Lancaster (and Halifax) photos is the two small circles fitted to the bomb aimer's blister. These first appeared in late June 1944 and remained until the end of the war. They were in fact, infra-red lamps which could flash a morse-code letter or remain constantly lit to identify the aircraft as friendly to other bombers that were fitted with AGLT (Airborne Gun Laying in Turrets), code named 'Village Inn'.
This system, fitted to the rear turret, detected any aircraft following behind the AGLT equipped Lancaster and allowed the gunner to automatically acquire the target aircraft by simply lining up a 'blip' in the centre of his gunsight. The gunner then had to check through an infra-red viewfinder to see if he could see the two 'Z' rings. If none were seen then the aircraft could be presumed hostile and engaged. This of course all then depended on the entire bomber force being fitted with the 'Z' Equipment rings as quickly as possible, which was mainly carried out in July 1944. The first operational trials of AGLT took place in the same month and by all accounts it worked well. However, by the end of the war, only a handful of squadrons had been equipped with this remarkably advanced weapon system.
**Inset photo shows an AGLT equipped rear turret on an early Lincoln bomber.*

THE HERCULES ENGINED MKII

The Bristol Hercules powered Lancaster was designed to meet an anticipated shortage of Rolls-Royce Merlin engines. Although this shortage never materialised, Armstrong-Whitworth fulfilled the contract to produce 300 machines, the first of which entered service in January 1943. 115 Squadron became the first unit to be fully equipped with the MkII and operated the type alongside 514, 408, 426 and 432 Squadrons during the campaigns of 1943. By the end of the year, production of the MkII had been terminated as Merlins were in plentiful supply and the Hercules powerplants were now needed for the new Halifax MkIII. Consequently, in the first half of 1944, the three Canadian squadrons converted to this new Halifax variant and 115 and 514 Sqn returned to Merlin powered Lancasters. Of the 300 MkIIs that entered service, over 60% were lost on operations, probably more of a reflection of the dark period it operated in rather than any shortcomings in its operational performance.

Above: DS604 was the fourth production MKII and was briefly on the charge of 61 Squadron before being passed on to 115 Squadron. The early MkIIs displayed the typical early Lancaster features such as 'Special Night' paint, light coloured frames in the turrets and a full set of fuselage windows. These windows were often painted over in service before being deleted entirely in production from the second half of 1943.
Also just visible in this photo is the large (Gee) whip aerial fitted in the rear of the cockpit canopy. This is another feature of early Lancasters, later models had two smaller whip aerials on the fuselage spine.
DS604 was also different from most MkIIs in that she (at this stage) wasn't fitted with spinners and she had the extended air intakes on top of the engines (see inset photo).
Below: The first 27 MkIIs were fitted with Hercules IV engines, the remainder such as DS771 seen here, with Hercules XVIs. Note the shorter air intakes on top of the engines.

THE TYPE 464 PROVISIONING

Above: The Type 464 (Provisioning) is now more commonly known as the 'Dambuster' Lancaster. Twenty-three examples were taken from the standard MkIII production line and modified to carry Barnes Wallis's 'Bouncing Bomb' codenamed 'Upkeep'. The main modification was the removal of the bomb doors and installation of two heavy cast-aluminium arms and a motor and drive-belt to hold and spin the weapon. The mid-upper turret was removed to save weight. The 'provisioning' meant that the modifications were temporary and the aircraft could be converted back to a standard MkIII, which indeed some of them were.

THE B1 SPECIAL

Above: The B1 Special was another variant designed specifically to carry one of Barnes Wallis's weapons; this time the 22,000lb Grand Slam. To save weight, the front and sometimes mid-upper turrets were removed as well as a lot of internal equipment including radios. Thus they generally flew with just a crew of five, leaving the Wireless Operator and Mid-Upper gunner at home. Also featured were treaded tyres and strengthened undercarriage legs and of course, uprated Merlin 24 engines. 32 examples were produced.

THE RARE MKVI

Above: The MkVI was a re-engined MkIII incorporating the more powerful Merlin 85 or 87 engine. This powerplant needed additional cooling, hence the wider radiators. Only nine were produced for service trials and five of them saw action towards the end of the war.

AERIALS AND APPENDAGES

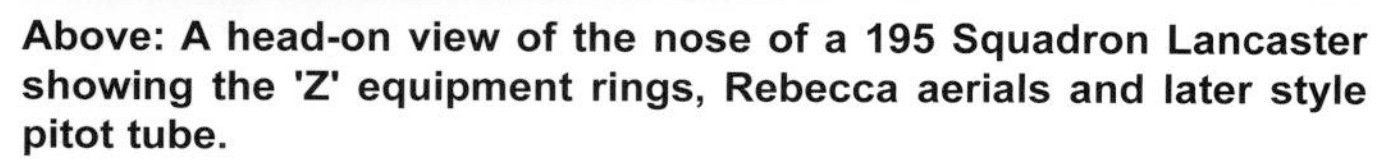

Above: A head-on view of the nose of a 195 Squadron Lancaster showing the 'Z' equipment rings, Rebecca aerials and later style pitot tube.

Top right and right: *Window* boxes appeared on Lancasters from late 1943 onwards. These strange shaped boxes were installed for the crews to be able to eject thousands of strips of tinfoil, (codenamed *'Window'*)* into the bomber stream which had the effect of 'blinding' German radar screens. First used in July 1943, the original plan was for the crews to push the bundles of *Window* down the flare chute. However, as this was positioned half way down the fuselage, it proved impractical, especially if the aircraft was manoeuvering at the time. *See page 97.
The solution was to cut a hole in the fuselage wall, usually under the nose on the starboard side as seen here, so that the bomb aimer could do the job with minimal effort. The aircraft on the right, HK593 JN-X of 75 Squadron is unusual in that it has an extra box fitted in the Flight Engineer's position.

Below: Another late modification to the Lancaster was the enlarged astrodome as seen here on this 195 Squadron aircraft. The standard size can been seen on the inset photo.

Above: The little silver coloured aerial fitted to the starboard side of the fuselage underneath the entrance door was an IFF (Identification Friend or Foe) aerial, the large bulge in front of it was the streamlined fairing for the H2S scanner*. The front section was painted black but the rear section was usually left transparent so that the downward identification lights could be seen.
*** see page 89**

Above: The 'towel rail' aerial under the fuselage on the port side was the Beam Approach aerial based on the Lorenz system which enabled pilots to carry out landings in poor visibility. This was replaced in 1944 by the Rebecca/Eureka system which was far more precise, (see the Rebecca aerials opposite).

Right: Warrant Officer Jimmy Huck stands next to the rear turret of his Lancaster. The prominent double chevron aerial next to him is the Monica aerial. This system transmitted pulses to the rear of the aircraft to help detect any potential fighters following behind. Unfortunately, German fighters were soon able to home in on these pulses and Monica was quickly withdrawn when this was discovered.

Left: This streamlined intake above the wing root is an extra cabin air intake, introduced late in the war presumably to provide extra cooling inside the fuselage which could become very hot during daylight operations. This was probably inspired by the switch to daylight ops and the prospect of Lancasters operating in the Far East. Even today, the BBMF Lancaster frequently flies with one of the fuselage escape hatches open to keep the temperatures bearable!

Below: The two escape hatches are clearly visible here on top of the fuselage, the dark dots are the windows in the hatches.
The black object sticking out from under the roundel is the fairing for the trailing aerial. This was moved quite early on in the production line to a position just under the port wing's leading edge, (see below left). The trailing aerial was nearly 300ft of wire on a winch which could be rolled out into the slipstream and connected to various radio and navigation devices.

GUN TURRETS

There were four main types of rear turret fitted to Lancasters during WWII. Most Lancasters had the FN20 (seen left) which was fitted with 4 x .303 Browning machine guns. On early examples, the internal framing was painted in a very light colour but by 1943 it had been painted black as seen here. This turret was slowly refined and improved into the FN120 which was introduced in late 1944. These two turrets were by far the most common and were found on over 90% of wartime Lancasters.

The FN82 rear turret was introduced on the MkVII Lancaster in 1945 and had higher calibre twin .5 Browning machine guns, as seen (opposite page top left) on NX611 at East Kirkby.

The Rose-Rice turret (opposite page top right) also had twin .5 Browning machine guns and was possibly the best turret of all. However only a few hundred examples were produced and they were all retro fitted to squadrons near to the Rose factory in Gainsborough.

The refinements made to the FN20 can be seen in the photos above and below The early FN20 (above) had no 'rear' windows (1) next to the gunner's shoulders. It also had more a extensive internal framework, note the horizontal bars (2 and 3) and the extra vertical frame (4). All of these are not visible in the later style turret (below) which also has the sliding panel (5) and external frame (6).

The central perspex was also slowly cut away during service as many gunners preferred the better visibility over the marginal warmth that the perspex provided. The turret above has a smaller hole directly in front of the gunner whereas the turret below has the entire centre section of perspex removed. The funnel shaped pieces on the end of the guns are flash eliminators to help preserve the gunner's night-vision.

Right: The mid-upper turret changed very little throught the wartime career of the Lancaster. The standard fitting was the FN50 seen here, fitted with 2 x .303 Browning machine guns. From March 1942, the turret was enclosed in an aerodynamic fairing on the production line so only a few very early examples flew without it (see page 29).

Below: The Austin built Lancaster MkVII was designed to have the electrically operated Martin mid-upper turret instead of the FN50. The biggest recognition feature of this turret was its placement further forward on the fuselage, just behind the wing-root in place of the aft escape hatch. This turret, equipped with twin .5 Browning machine guns, was also fitted to over 200 of the later Canadian MkXs as in this example illustrated.

Below: Early Lancasters were fitted with an FN64 ventral turret including this example R5727 which flew to Canada to become the pattern aircraft for the Canadian built MkXs. However, the FN64 proved ineffective operationally so most Lancasters flew without any defensive armament under the aircraft. Later in 1944 some squadrons did experiment with installing a single .5 calibre, hand held machine gun in the hatch left by the deleted turret, but again its effect was minimal.

Above: The nose turret remained the same throughout the war. The FN5 was equipped with 2 x .303 Browning machine guns each one loaded with 1000 rounds of ammunition. This turret was rarely used as night fighters tended not to carry out head-on attacks! The only time it was permanently manned was on low level raids such as Operation Chastise (The Dambuster Raid) when the guns were loaded with 100% tracer ammunition to provide an impressive stream of fire to keep the flak gunners' heads down.

INSIDE THE LANCASTER

Although the Lancaster changed very little externally, the situation inside was quite different with many new pieces of kit and instruments being added or moved around throughout its service life. This instrument panel is that of NX611 a preserved MKVII at East Kirkby. Numbered are some of the basic essentials common to every Lancaster.

1. The blind-flying panel of 6 main instruments common to all aircraft.
2. The Direction Finding indicator.
3. The pilot had two compasses, the main one by his knee and a smaller one on top of the panel.
4. The four main throttle controls for the engines.
5. The propeller speed control levers.
6. The main ignition switches.
7. The four engine boost and RPM gauges.
8. Propeller feathering buttons.
9. Fire extinguisher buttons.
10. Passage to bomb-aimer's position.
11. Flap selection handle.
12. Undercarriage selection lever (partly hidden).
13. The pilot's armour-plated headrest.
14. The cockpit escape hatch.
15. Elevator trim control.

Unlike some other RAF bombers, the Lancaster was designed just to have one pilot who sat on the left. The space on the right was occupied by the Flight Engineer who had a fold-down seat if required. His instruments were mounted on the starboard side of the fuselage and were mainly fuel, oil and coolant gauges.
Here F/O Burnside of 619 Squadron reaches back to switch on the fuel contents gauges on his panel.

Right and below: The navigator sat just behind the pilot's seat under the cockpit coaming facing the port side of the aircraft. He had a curtain that could close him off from the cockpit to allow him to use a light and to avoid being distracted by the general mayhem going on outside the aircraft over the target area. His small rectangular window was also deleted on later models to provide total seclusion.
He had copies of some of the pilot's instruments in front of him and later in the war also had various navigation aids such as Gee and H_2S.
In the photo below you can see the little known sheet of armoured glass (15) bolted above the navigator's position to protect the flight engineer from a stern attack.

Above: The wireless operator sat facing forward just aft of the navigator on the port side of the fuselage. He had the cockpit astrodome just above his head and the main wingspar just behind him. He also had the luxury of the main cabin heat outlet nearby so rarely wore more than battledress, even on the coldest nights! In this view facing forward, the navigator's seat is just to the right of the W/Op's right hand, the cockpit beyond that.

Left: Dambuster bomb-aimer George 'Johnny' Johnson revisits his old position in NX611. He is standing in the open forward escape hatch which was the recommended parachute exit for all of the crew if time permitted. There was no specific seat provided for the bomb-aimer (or air-bomber as he was officially known) and many of them knelt or lay prone for the duration of the flight. For take off and landings they were supposed to leave the nose area for safety but many didn't.

Johnny's left hand rests on the redesigned oval window. The yellow bar in the bottom right of the photo is one of many solid hand rails throughout the aircraft to help crew members move through the aircraft without grabbing some more sensitive instrument or lever by mistake. Another two of these rails can be seen in the photo above.

CAMOUFLAGE AND MARKINGS

NATIONAL MARKINGS

The national markings changed just once on wartime Lancasters; in July 1942. The early war equally sized fuselage roundel, (below left) was replaced by the modified version (below right) which cut down the size of the white and yellow portions and increased the blue and red. This was to reduce its visibility, particularly at night. The same principle was applied to the fin flashes where the white part was reduced significantly. The upper wing roundels remained just blue and red throughout the war.

UP TO JULY 1942

AUGUST 1942 - 1947

CAMOUFLAGE PATTERNS

The uppersurface camouflage pattern remained unchanged throughout the Lancaster's wartime career as can be seen in these two views of an early MkI (bottom) and a B1 Special (below). The only variations were the tops of the engine cowlings which sometimes were finished in one colour, either dark green or dark earth. The black lines on the wings indicate the extent of the area within which it is safe for the groundcrew to walk. The lighter coloured square on the starboard wing root is the dinghy hatch which was frequently sealed with red tape

The undersides were always finished in black which extended up the sides of the fuselage to a point just over the top of the wing. Fins were black. The only exception was the B1 Special (below) which was given its own unique daylight scheme of a lighter green and earth uppersurfaces, extending down the fuselage sides and including the fins, with sky undersurfaces. The black outer fin colour on this particular aircraft is believed to be a formation leader's tactical marking.

CODE LETTERS

Up until July 1942, all identification letters were applied in grey paint. From August 1942 until the end of the war this was changed to dull red to match the serial number. Each squadron was allocated a two letter code, eg 'AA' for 75 Squadron, which was painted usually, (but not always*), to the left of the fuselage roundel. Each aircraft was then allocated an individual aircraft letter which was painted on the other side of the roundel.

With the expansion of the bombing offensive, many squadrons found themselves with more aircraft than letters of the alphabet so either a horizontal bar or, more commonly, a small 2 was added above the individual code letter. Eventually a second set of code letters was allocated to some of the larger squadrons, in 75 Squadron's case 'JN', and these aircraft were generally operated as 'C' Flight. Many new squadrons were then formed from the 'C' Flights of existing squadrons. With this expansion also came the need to include numbers into the squadron codes as all permutations of letters had been used. Therefore many squadrons formed in 1944 such as 227 Sqn (9J) and 635 Sqn (F2) received an alpha-numeric combination.

*see 101 Squadron page 54.

Below: PD235 UL-N^{2} wears standard late war codes and markings with the letters in dull red. Note the small 2 after the N indicating there was already a UL-N on the squadron.

THE FIRST MONTHS OF PEACE

Right: Within weeks of the end of hostilities in Europe many young pilots were expressing their joy by indulging in a bit of carefree low flying! To discourage this, the squadron code letters were repainted white and the aircraft serial number was painted in large white numerals underneath the wings as shown here on PP687 KM-W of 44 Squadron.

Bottom right: Also at around this time, Lancasters were rolling off the production line in a new scheme designed for operations in the Far East against Japan. Standard black undersurfaces were worn but the entire fuselage sides and uppersurfaces were painted white to help keep the airframe, and those inside it, cool. This 7 Squadron example TW660, one of the last Lancasters to roll off the production line has an FN82 rear turret fitted as standard. Keen eyes will spot that the upper wing roundel now has a white ring between the blue and red, another feature introduced at the end of the war.

TACTICAL MARKINGS

With the diminishing threat from Luftwaffe fighters, as Allied Forces swarmed into France after D-Day the night bombers once again started to operate in daylight, sometimes in huge waves of hundreds of aircraft. It was important for squadrons to keep together within the force but it was found that the dull red code letters were useless for squadron identification even at close range. At first, many squadrons tried adding a yellow outline to squadron codes and sometimes repeating the codes on the tailplane. This had a positive effect, but to further enhance aerial recognition, an informal system of fin markings then evolved, each squadron having a different combination of colour and pattern. These markings first appeared in June 1944 and reached a peak in October 1944. They were generally applied to senior crews' aircraft and usually consisted of red, white or black symbols being applied over contrasting backgrounds. 5 Group seems to have been the most active with nearly all squadrons having some form of painted fins at some point. 1 Group also had some colourful examples, using blue, white and yellow paint on not just the fins but also the wingtips and fuselage on occasions.

3 Group came up with two yellow bars on the fin to signify a Gee-H equipped Lancaster. This precision bombing equipment allowed the aircraft to bomb with reasonable accuracy through cloud. As such, non Gee-H equipped Lancasters were instructed to formate upon a Lancaster sporting the two yellow bars and bomb when it did.

Above: 1 Group's 166 Squadron displayed yellow fins on some of their aircraft in 1944.

Above: DX-Y RA530 of 57 Squadron illustrates nicely the yellow outlined codes and the fin markings, in this case black stripe on a red background.
Below: This 467 Squadron Lancaster has a blue or black cross on a white fin, note the fin-flash is retained.

Above: This design was painted on PB842 of 619 Sqn, 5 Group.

Below: This 630 Squadron Lancaster has a red fin and black rudder.

Above: The two yellow bars as seen on many 3 Group aircraft indicating a Gee-H Leader.

THE SQUADRONS

7 SQUADRON

8 (PFF) GROUP

Code Letters

MG

and XU (C Flt)

Operated the Lancaster from July 1943 - August 1949

Wartime Base
Oakington

Raids flown with Lancasters
279

Lancasters lost
87 plus 20 in accidents

Points of Interest
Flew the Stirling for nearly three years before converting to Lancasters. Became one of the original Pathfinder squadrons and, with 35 Squadron, introduced H2S into operational service.

Above: POWs line up with the crew of PB437 MG-G at Lubeck as they prepare to go home on the 10th May 1945. Many Lancaster squadrons took part in POW repatriation flights at the end of the war, codenamed Operation Exodus.

Below: PB118 was one of many Lancasters on 7 Squadron that had the MG squadron codes painted considerably smaller than the code letter. This was a common feature on the unit's Stirlings earlier in the war.

Below: 'Flash' McCollah (centre) and his crew pose in front of Lancaster 'G' George, a veteran of 80 ops when this photo was taken.

9 SQUADRON

5 GROUP

Code Letters

WS

Operated the Lancaster from August 1942 - July 1946

Wartime Bases
Waddington
4/43 Bardney

Raids flown with Lancasters
301

Lancasters lost
111 plus 22 in accidents

Points of Interest
One of the few bomber squadrons to be operational throughout the war, 9 Squadron was also the only unit to join 617 Squadron in many of their precision bombing raids of 1944/1945, including the sinking of the Tirpitz on 12th November 1944.

Although of poor quality, this photo is interesting as it shows a very early MkI, note the light framing in the rear turret and the original positioned trailing aerial fairing just behind the roundel. The smaller letter 'Z' is also of note as is the lack of exhaust shrouds on the camera aircraft.

Left: Flying Officer A E Manning and his crew disembark from W4964 WS-J at Bardney, in the early hours of 6th January 1944, after a raid on Stettin, Germany. This aircraft can also be seen below. The individual code letter 'J' was painted smaller in the same style as the 'Z' coded aircraft at the top of the page.

Right: 9 Squadron's Lancasters displayed some of the most interesting nose art in Bomber Command. This is the famous WS-J W4964 'Johnnie Walker' a veteran of 106 ops, all with 9 Squadron. The figure and motto are based upon the famous 'Johnnie Walker' Whisky brand. The bomb tally is fascinating as it includes to the left, various symbols relating to the aircraft's history. These include four DFM ribbons two DFC ribbons, a chevron representing a year's service, a swastika, presumably indicating a downed fighter, a searchlight denoting one shot out by a gunner and a red star probably representing one of the Tirpitz raids to Russia. The kangaroo painted below the navigator's window was added to represent Flt Lt Melrose's Aussie navigator F/O Jimmy Moore.

Pictured left is 'Naughty Nan', possibly DV161 whilst serving with 9 Squadron. This aircraft has a rare combination of the shallow bomb-aimer's blister and 'Z' Equipment rings, dating the picture to around summer 1944.

Seen below and at the bottom of the page is 'Lonesome Lola?' LL845 WS-L, another 9 Squadron veteran with an eventual tally of 97 ops. The yellow outlined codes were introduced in the summer of 1944 to help with identification as Bomber Command started to take part in daylight raids.

FLIGHT SERGEANT GEORGE THOMPSON VC

On 1st January 1945, 9 Squadron was detailed to take part in a daylight raid on the Dortmund-Ems Canal.

24 year old Flt Sgt Thompson was a wireless operator in one of the Lancasters when, immediately after the bombing run, his aircraft was hit by flak just in front of the mid-upper turret. The fuselage immediately filled with flames and Thompson saw that the mid-upper gunner was unconscious in the blazing turret. He battled through the flames and managed to drag the gunner clear and extinguish his burning clothing with his bare hands. Severely burnt himself, Thompson then noticed that the rear gunner was also trapped and unconscious in the flames. Again he went back and extracted the gunner and again he extinguished his burning clothing with his bare hands.

Thompson then crawled forward through the badly holed fuselage and reported the situation to the pilot. Such were his injuries, including by now frost-bite, that the pilot couldn't recognise his valiant wireless operator. The aircraft crash landed some 40 minutes later and Thompson was rushed to hospital. Sadly, he died three weeks later of his injuries, as did one of the gunners. For his brave and selfless actions, Thompson was awarded the Victoria Cross.

12 SQUADRON

1 GROUP

Code Letters

PH

and GZ (C Flt)

Operated the Lancaster from Nov 1942 - August 1946

Wartime Base
Wickenby

Raids flown with Lancasters
309

Lancasters lost
111
plus 18 in accidents

Points of Interest
Served throughout the war as a bomber squadron and incurred the second highest percentage losses in Bomber Command.

Above: ND342 PH-U is fitted with a Rose rear turret and H_2S. She was lost on 12th December 1944. The light coloured circle on the nose is a gas detection patch, common on 1 Group aircraft*.
see page 98

Above: Lancaster W4366 PH-R standing at dispersal at Wickenby. Note the unusual positioning of the code letters and the re-positioned serial number, a unique feature of many early 12 Squadron Lancasters.

Below: Later in the war, the code letters were applied in a more conventional fashion as seen here.

15 SQUADRON

3 GROUP

Code Letters

LS

and DJ (C Flt)

Operated the Lancaster from Dec 1943 - February 1947

Wartime Base
Mildenhall

Raids flown with Lancasters
226

Lancasters lost
45
plus 11 in crashes

Points of Interest
Served throughout the war as a bomber squadron and spent nearly three years flying the Stirling before eventually converting to Lancasters.

Top Right: Some Lancasters lasted longer than others. This is a 134 op veteran LL806 seen here post-war with her serial number painted under the wings and white script style code letters. Some squadrons used the orders to re-colour the codes at the end of the war to introduce a more flamboyant typeface!

Above Right: A nice air to air showing ME844 LS-C shortly after being delivered to the squadron in June 1944.

Right: ME844 a year later, now sporting the identity letter 'W' and many more mission symbols along with the post-war white codes.

Below: A Gee-H leader LS-Y comes into land at Mildenhall in front of the control tower on runway 22.

At the end of the war, 15 Squadron inherited the Lancaster B1 Specials that had been flown by 617 Squadron to deliver the huge Grand Slam bombs over Germany. These aircraft were stripped down as much as possible to enable them to carry the huge 22,000lb bomb. As such, without the bomb, they were the 'Formula One' version of the Lancaster and great fun to fly! The squadron used the aircraft to take part in Operation Front Line, a combined exercise with US B-29s dropping Grand Slams and Tallboys on the U-Boat pens at Farge, near Bremen.

Top right and right: A bit of formation practice for the B1 Specials, LS-Z seen through the prop arc of the camera aircraft and LS-Y and LS-O photographed from the rear turret.

Below right: Wing Commander 'Tubby' Baker who completed 100 ops, poses with his crew in front of PD127 LS-S, ex YZ-F of 617 Squadron. Note the Grand Slam bomb slung underneath the aircraft.

Below: Another B1 Special LS-X, this one is unusual in that the mid-upper fairing has been retained.

35

(MADRAS PRESIDENCY)

SQUADRON

8 (PFF) GROUP

Code Letters

TL

Operated the Lancaster from
March 1944 - Sept 1949

Wartime Base
Graveley

Raids flown with Lancasters
202

Lancasters lost
27
plus 6 in crashes

Points of Interest
Flew the Halifax for well over three years before converting to Lancasters. Became one of the original Pathfinder squadrons and, with 7 Squadron, introduced H2S into operational service.

Top and below: Post war photos of 35 Squadron displaying their fresh batch of Lancasters for the camera. The aircraft are finished in the white/black 'Tiger Force' scheme which was formulated for use in the war against Japan. TW659 below was a MkI (FE), the FE standing for Far East and indicating that it had been modified for operations in tropical conditions.
The view below nicely illustrates the significant rearward lean to the main undercarriage legs which is often overlooked by modellers and artists.

Above: Wing Commander Nicholls DFC and his PFF crew of Peters, Sculk, Sparks, Jenkins, Monk and Jones line up for the camera with an unmarked Lancaster in 1945.

44
(RHODESIA)
SQUADRON

5 GROUP

Code Letters

KM

Operated the Lancaster from
Dec 1941 - Sept 1947

Wartime Bases
Waddington,
6/43 Dunholme Lodge
10/44 Spilsby

Raids flown with Lancasters
299

Lancasters lost
149
plus 21 in accidents

Points of Interest
One of only two squadrons to have served with Bomber Command from the beginning to the end of World War II.
Introduced the Lancaster to operational service and consequently suffered the heaviest Lancaster losses in Bomber Command.
Sqn Ldr J D Nettleton was awarded the VC with this squadron for his part in the Augsburg Raid on 17th April 1942.

Above: A nice study of L7578 KM-B practicing for the Augsburg Raid in April 1942. It is believed that this aircraft was on loan from 97 Squadron at the time. It was one of the first Lancasters to be produced, note the unfaired mid-upper turret.

Right: A rigger puts the finishing touches to the bar above the 'O' on R5540 KM-O. Later in the war, the bar would signify a second aircraft with that code letter on the squadron, however on this occasion it probably identifies this Lancaster as belonging to the unit's conversion flight.

Below: Airborne for the press probably on the same day, 29th September 1942, are: W4162 KM-Y, flown by Pilot Officer T G Hackney, W4125 KM-W, flown by Sergeant C Watt and W4187 KM-S, flown by Pilot Officer J Stephens DFM, who was killed with his crew two nights later over Wismar.

Right: The morning after the night before. The daylight of 18th August 1943 reveals the extent of the damage to Lancaster ED611 KM-J, sustained over Peenemunde by the guns of a night fighter. The starboard outer was badly damaged, note the feathered prop and the holed flap. The fuselage also sustained hits, two 20mm cannon shell holes can clearly be seen in the photo below. Despite this and further strikes, Pilot Officer Aldridge brought his aircraft and crew back safely to Dunholme Lodge. ED611 was subsequently repaired and continued on ops for the remainder of the war. Note how the squadron codes have been painted over the windows.

Below: A couple of months before ED611 sustained her damage she was part of the 'Shuttle Raid' force that bombed Friedrichshafen. Three days later on the 23rd June 1943, the force flew back, bombing La Spezia on the way. Here, in this rare photo, ED611 is about to set off from Blida on the long journey home.

SQUADRON LEADER JOHN DERING NETTLETON VC

In June 1941, John Dering Nettleton was posted to 44 Squadron as a Flight Commander. This experienced South African had already completed two tours and along with his fellow squadron members now faced the challenge of introducing the Lancaster to operational service. One of the first 'showpiece' raids was planned for the 17th April 1942 where a force of 12 Lancasters, (six from 44 and six from 97 Squadron), would carry out an audacious low level strike on the MAN diesel engine factory in Augsburg, southern Germany. The 44 Squadron section hit trouble shortly after crossing the French coast. A large formation of Me109s returning from another interception, spotted the unescorted bombers and immediately gave chase. One by one, the vulnerable Lancasters were picked off, four being shot down, the other two, Nettleton's included, being hit repeatedly.

Despite this Nettleton and Garwell in the other surviving Lanc pressed on and attacked the target amidst intense flak. This flak claimed Garwell's aircraft over the target, leaving Nettleton and his crew to make their own way back to the UK, eventually landing in Blackpool some 10 hours after leaving Waddington.

For his unflinching determination, valour and leadership in this raid, John Nettleton was awarded the VC.

After a brief spell instructing with 1661 HCU, the now Wing Commander Nettleton returned to 44 Squadron as C/O in January 1943.

Tragically, the man whose bravery had helped to establish the Lancaster legend was also to die in a Lancaster. On 13th July 1943 his aircraft failed to return from a raid on Turin.

Right: The crew of ED331 disembark after a long and stressful night over Berlin, 2nd March 1943.

Below: Four powerful Merlins disturb the peaceful night air at Dunholme Lodge as KM-A R5729 prepares to head for Berlin on 2nd January 1944. Less than two week later she was lost over Brunswick with all her crew.

Left: A short sunshine break. Another 'Shuttle Raid' photo this time depicting one of 49 Squadron's Lancs, ED426 EA-P sitting in the scrubland at Blida. She was destined to be lost on a cold night over Stuttgart, 8th October 1943, just a few months after this photograph was taken.

Below: The bulk of the Lancaster is clearly illustrated in this photograph of a WAAF driver, LACW Lilian Yule, towing DV238 EA-O at Fiskerton, summer 1943. The low morning light picks out some great details such as the mass balance on the elevator trim tab and the aerial wires leading from the cockpit to the fins, note where the attachment point is on the fin.

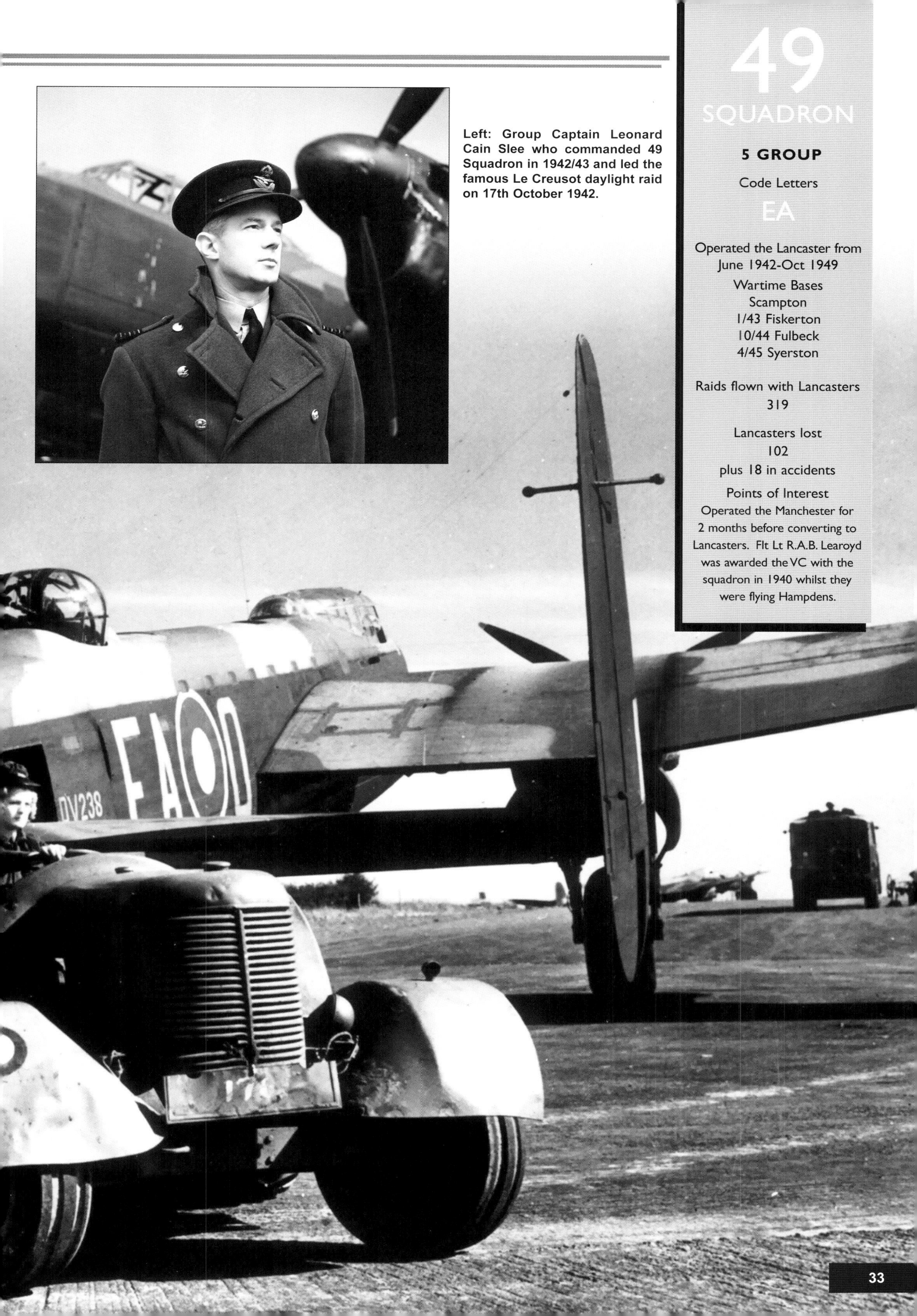

Left: Group Captain Leonard Cain Slee who commanded 49 Squadron in 1942/43 and led the famous Le Creusot daylight raid on 17th October 1942.

49 SQUADRON

5 GROUP

Code Letters

EA

Operated the Lancaster from June 1942-Oct 1949

Wartime Bases
Scampton
1/43 Fiskerton
10/44 Fulbeck
4/45 Syerston

Raids flown with Lancasters
319

Lancasters lost
102
plus 18 in accidents

Points of Interest

Operated the Manchester for 2 months before converting to Lancasters. Flt Lt R.A.B. Learoyd was awarded the VC with the squadron in 1940 whilst they were flying Hampdens.

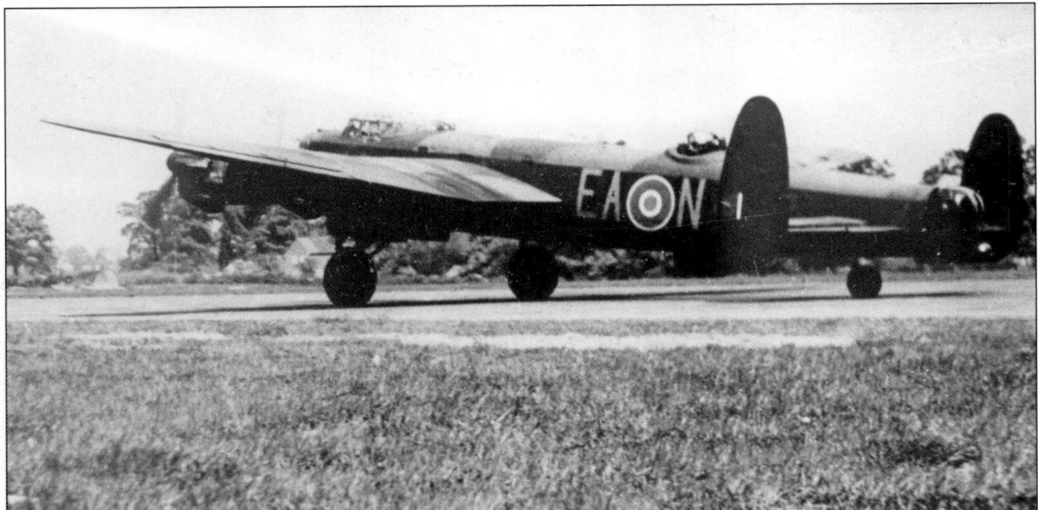

Above: At peace. A beautiful photograph of 49 Squadron Lancasters at rest, the lack of activity around the aircraft would suggest that there are no ops tonight.

Left: A fairly anonymous EA-N taxies past the camera, probably in 1943.

Below: Lancaster EA-H takes off from Blida on the second leg of the shuttle raid, another Lanc can be seen climbing just ahead of the mid-upper turret.

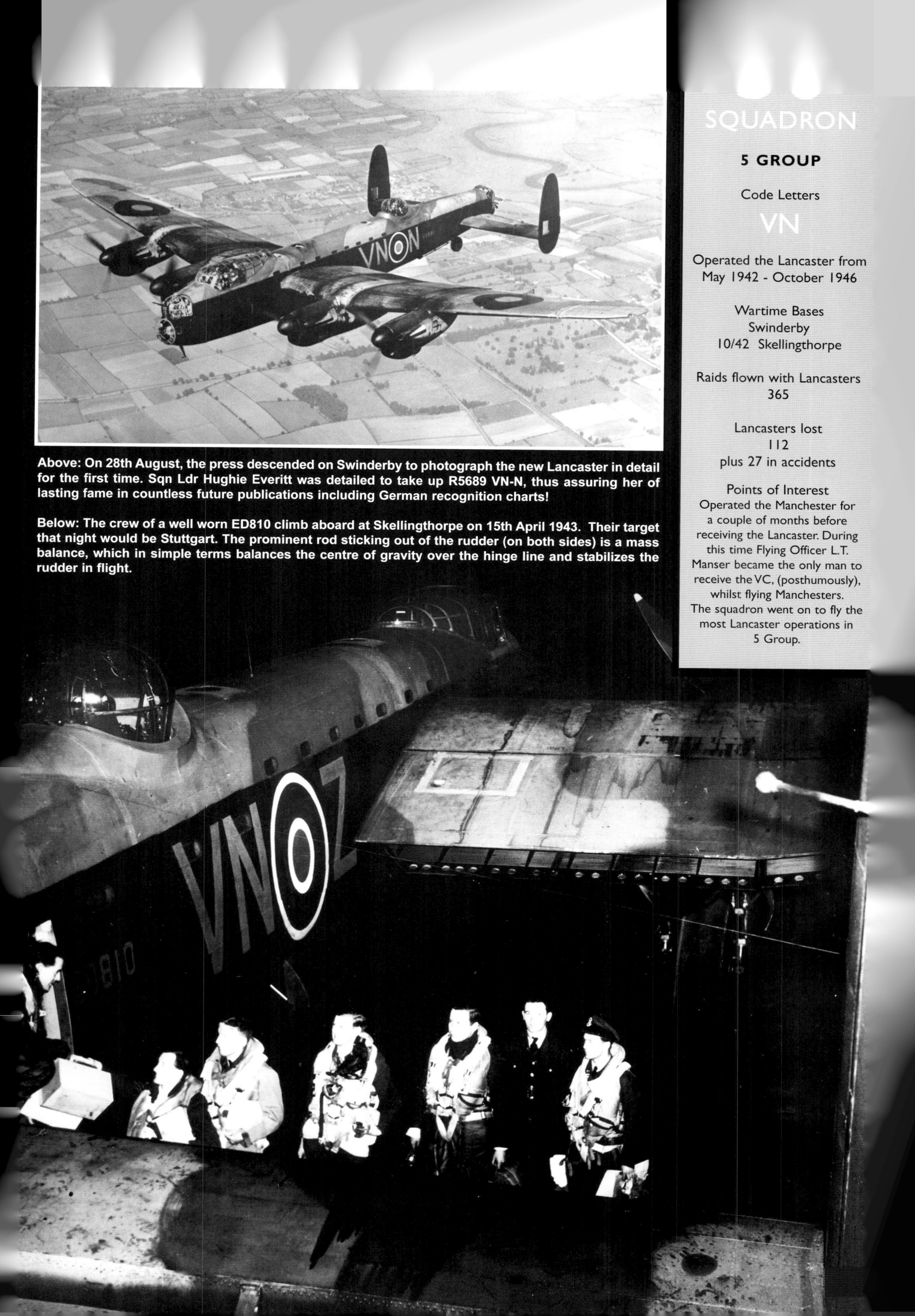

SQUADRON

5 GROUP

Code Letters

VN

Operated the Lancaster from May 1942 - October 1946

Wartime Bases
Swinderby
10/42 Skellingthorpe

Raids flown with Lancasters
365

Lancasters lost
112
plus 27 in accidents

Points of Interest
Operated the Manchester for a couple of months before receiving the Lancaster. During this time Flying Officer L.T. Manser became the only man to receive the VC, (posthumously), whilst flying Manchesters. The squadron went on to fly the most Lancaster operations in 5 Group.

Above: On 28th August, the press descended on Swinderby to photograph the new Lancaster in detail for the first time. Sqn Ldr Hughie Everitt was detailed to take up R5689 VN-N, thus assuring her of lasting fame in countless future publications including German recognition charts!

Below: The crew of a well worn ED810 climb aboard at Skellingthorpe on 15th April 1943. Their target that night would be Stuttgart. The prominent rod sticking out of the rudder (on both sides) is a mass balance, which in simple terms balances the centre of gravity over the hinge line and stabilizes the rudder in flight.

Left: A crew pose with Lancaster VN-K R5691, the cartoon king nose art is probably Old King Cole a reference to the pilot T B Cole. The aircraft, one of the first 200 originally ordered as Manchesters but built as Lancasters*, lasted just over three months on the squadron. She failed to return from a raid on Milan on 4th October 1942. The parachute symbols under the bomb symbols are for mine-laying operations.

**The early serialled Lancasters in the R and W range were all originally ordered as Manchesters hence the reason why the prototype had a 'later' serial number in the BT range. (RAF serials went from A-Z followed by 4 numerals and then AA to ZZ followed by 3 numerals).*

Below: The crew of PB739 pose for the camera at Skellingthorpe in 1945. L-R; J Saunders, H Griffin, D Taylor DFM, T Mackay, J Oldacre. Back; G Gardner, A Bartlett.

Of interest is the hyphen in the serial number, a very unusual feature. Also visible is the external dinghy release handle and associated stencilling. There was also an internal release cord for the dinghy that ran along the fuselage roof as well as an automatic immersion switch which released it when in contact with water.

Above: Another press photo of R5689 VN-N, flying in the hot summer air over Nottinghamshire. Note the forward escape hatch is open to allow some cool air into the sweltering fuselage. Also note that the national markings have recently been changed to the lower visibility versions and, as yet, the ground crew haven't painted the white stripe on the port tail fin.

Below: A nice air to air of VN-D taken on 12th September 1944. By this time, the squadron was taking part in occasional daylight raids and so had added a thin yellow outline to the codes to aid identification. As a further aid, the code letters were repeated on the upper surfaces of the tailplane, just visible in this view. This aircraft is also equipped with H2S and a Monica aerial under the rear turret.

57 SQUADRON

5 GROUP

Code Letters

DX

and QT (C Flt)

Operated the Lancaster from Sept 1942 - Nov 1945

Wartime Bases
Scampton
8/43 East Kirkby

Raids flown with Lancasters
348

Lancasters lost
108 plus 31 in accidents

Points of Interest
One of the few squadrons to serve in three different Groups during the war, suffering higher than average losses throughout.

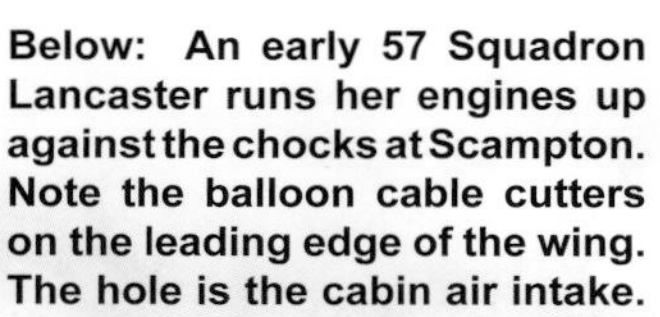

Below: An early 57 Squadron Lancaster runs her engines up against the chocks at Scampton. Note the balloon cable cutters on the leading edge of the wing. The hole is the cabin air intake.

Above: Another photo from Blida of the Shuttle Raid participants. This time W5008 DX-B of 57 Squadron which is believed to be have been borrowed by a 617 Squadron crew on this raid. Close examination of the print shows part of the trailing aerial hanging below the fuselage just at the front of the roundel.

Above: ED989 'Frederick III' the personal aircraft of the C/O, Wing Commander Frederick Campbell Hopcroft who commanded the squadron from September 1942 to July 1943.

Left: A DX coded Lancaster slips underneath the oil streaked starboard inner of another Lancaster in April 1944.

Below: As dusk gathers over Scampton, Lancasters of 57 Squadron await their crews.

61 SQUADRON

5 GROUP

Code Letters

QR

Operated the Lancaster from April 1942 - May 1946

Wartime Bases
Woolfox Lodge
5/42 Syerston
11/43 Skellingthorpe
1/44 Coningsby
4/44 Skellingthorpe

Raids flown with Lancasters
376

Lancasters lost
116 plus 25 in accidents

Points of Interest
Flew more raids with the Lancaster than any other squadron in Bomber Command. Flt Lt. W. Reid was awarded the VC for his actions on the night of 3rd November 1943.

Above: The tireless groundcrews line up for a photo in front of QR-H in summer 1944. Note that 'H' appears to have had a 'nose job', receiving an entirely new nose forward of the cockpit.

Below: Probably the most famous 61 Sqn Lancaster, EE176 QR-M 'Mickey the Moocher' which notched up over 120 ops.

Below: An unidentified crew walk to their aircraft at Syerston. Lancasters were nearly always parked with bomb-doors open, as opening them without engine power involved a serious amount of hand pumping for about 15 minutes! They would be closed therefore only after the engines had been started.

Above: 61 Squadron also took part in the Shuttle Raids, here QR-B taxies through the dust and QR-R thunders down the runway, both at Blida.

Below: Another centurion Lanc on 61 Squadron was ED860 'N' . Here she receives her 100th bomb symbol in late June 1944. This is one of the earliest dated photos of a Lancaster fitted with 'Z' equipment in the bomb aimer's blister.

Above: LM360, the Lancaster in which Bill Reid won his VC. Delivered in summer 1943, this LM series Lancaster is one of the last to have factory installed fuselage windows.

FLIGHT LIEUTENANT WILLIAM REID VC

On the night of 3rd November 1943, Flt Lt Reid was flying Lancaster LM360 QR-O on a raid against Dusseldorf. Shortly after crossing the Dutch coast, the Lancaster was attacked by an Me110 night fighter. Reid suffered wounds to his head, shoulders and hands but he managed to shake off the fighter and decided to press on with his damaged but manageable aircraft. The odds, however, were stacked against them that night and soon after, a Focke Wulf 190 raked the crippled bomber with cannon fire. The navigator was killed and the wireless operator fatally wounded. The flight engineer was hit in the forearm and Reid was hit again. Despite all this and with the mid upper and rear turrets out of action, Reid continued his course and bombed the target some 50 minutes later.

The long journey home in the freezing, shattered cockpit took all of Reid's remaining strength and consciousness. Remarkably, with the gallant help of the flight engineer Sgt J W Norris, he got the aircraft back to England where he performed an emergency landing on the USAAF base at Shipdham. Reid was awarded the VC for 'tenacity and devotion to duty beyond praise'. Norris received the CGM.

After recovering from his injuries, Bill Reid returned to operations with 617 Sqn. On 31st July 1944 he was forced to bale out of his Lancaster when it was hit by falling bombs. He spent the rest of the war as a POW and died in December 2001.

Left: 30th July 1943 at Syerston and a typical Lancaster crew have their photograph taken with their aircraft and groundcrew, (usually done at the end of a tour of ops).
L-R Flying Officer F L Hewish, bomb aimer:
Pilot Officer W H Eager RCAF, pilot:
Sergeant F R Stone, wireless operator:
Sergeant L S Vanner, rear gunner:
Sergeant H T Petts, navigator:
Sergeant F R Sharrard, mid-upper gunner:
Sergeant L Lawrence, flight engineer.
Ground crew, (sitting) left to right:
Leading Aircraftsman W A Long, flight mechanic (engines):
Corporal Chaz Bowyer, fitter (later to become a well known aviation author):
Leading Aircraftsman J Blackwood, flight mechanic (airframe).

The Lancaster is W4236 QR-K.

75

(New Zealand)

SQUADRON

3 GROUP

Code Letters

AA

and JN (C Flt)

Operated the Lancaster from March 1944 - October 1945

Wartime Base
Mepal

Raids flown with Lancasters
208

Lancasters lost
47
plus 8 in accidents

Points of Interest
Formed in 1940 from the New Zealand Wellington Flight, the squadron was operating Stirlings up until March 1944. During the war as a whole it suffered the second highest casualties in Bomber Command.

Above and Left: A 'C' Flight crew and groundcrew pose with their aircraft JN-X HK593. The forty bomb symbols date these photos to around 9th February 1945. Although not visible in these photos, the aircraft had bulged bomb doors and on the port side the serial number was displayed with the HK above the 593. (See also page 9 for more photos of this aircraft).

Left: Although of poor quality, this is an interesting shot of LM625 AA-U. Note that the G-H bars on the fins are only on the outboard side

Lancaster AA-A photographed over the oil storage depot at Bec D'Ambes, France, 4th August 1944.

Above: PB421 AA-K was delivered to 75 Squadron in August 1944. Note that 75 Squadron placed the squadron code letters before or after the roundel, as can be seen with AA-P ND974 (left), photographed here just after the war on troop carrying duties.

83 SQUADRON

5 GROUP
8 (PFF) GROUP

Code Letters

OL

Operated the Lancaster from April 1942 - July 1946

Wartime Bases
Scampton
8/42 Wyton
4/44 Coningsby

Raids flown with Lancasters
306

Lancasters lost
91 plus 25 in accidents

Points of Interest

Operated throughout the war and became one of the original Pathfinder squadrons in 1942. Transferred back to 5 Group in May 1944 to operate as part of the Group's own marker force. Sgt. John Hannah was awarded the VC for his actions on the night of 15th November 1940 in an 83 Squadron Hampden.

Above: OL-F is a very early Lancaster, note the unfaired mid-upper turret, light frameworked turrets and matt black fuselage. She is however carrying the later style roundels and fin flashes which date the photo no earlier than June 1942.

Below: OL-M R5626 comes into land at Scampton probably summer 1942.

Below: 83 Squadron Lancasters taxi along a narrow perimeter track on a misty day making the airfield identification somewhat difficult!

Above: Scampton 25th June 1942. 83 Squadron lines up for take off on the third 1000 bomber raid against Bremen. The lead aircraft R5620 OL-H and her seven crewmen failed to return that night. One wonders if the unshrouded outer exhausts had anything to do with her demise.

Below: 83 Squadron Lancasters line up for an official visit on 22nd October 1942 at Wyton. The censor has removed the codes of the second Lancaster. Note the long Gee aerial at the rear of the cockpit, a common feature on early Lancasters.

Above: R5852 OL-Y cruises above the clouds in the summer of 1942. This side view nicely illustrates the dihedral of the Lancaster's wings in flight, the wingtips being well above the top of the fuselage.

Below and Right: It's a little known fact that the RAF Museum's famous Lancaster R5868 PO-S, started her operational life with 83 Sqn as OL-Q. These photos were taken in May 1943 and show her codes and 'Devils of the Air' nose art.

Right: F/O 'Rick' Garvey and his crew pose on R5868 OL-Q. L-R, F/S Bill Webster (Flt Eng), F/S Len Thomas (MU), F/S Turner (WO), P/O 'Jimmy' Sukthanker (Nav), F/O 'Rick' Garvey (P), F/S Jack Cooke (BA), P/O Hugh Ashton (RG).

90
SQUADRON

3 GROUP

Code Letters

WP

and XY (C Flt)

Operated the Lancaster from May 1944 - Dec 1947

Wartime Base
Tuddenham

Raids flown with Lancasters
181

Lancasters lost
25
plus 12 in accidents

Points of Interest
Had an eventful war, starting off as a training squadron before becoming the only RAF unit to operate the American B-17 Flying Fortress as a daylight bomber. The 'C' Flight went on to form 186 Squadron.

Above: 'Good Hunting Freddie' was LM588 WP-F which served on the squadron during the summer of 1944.

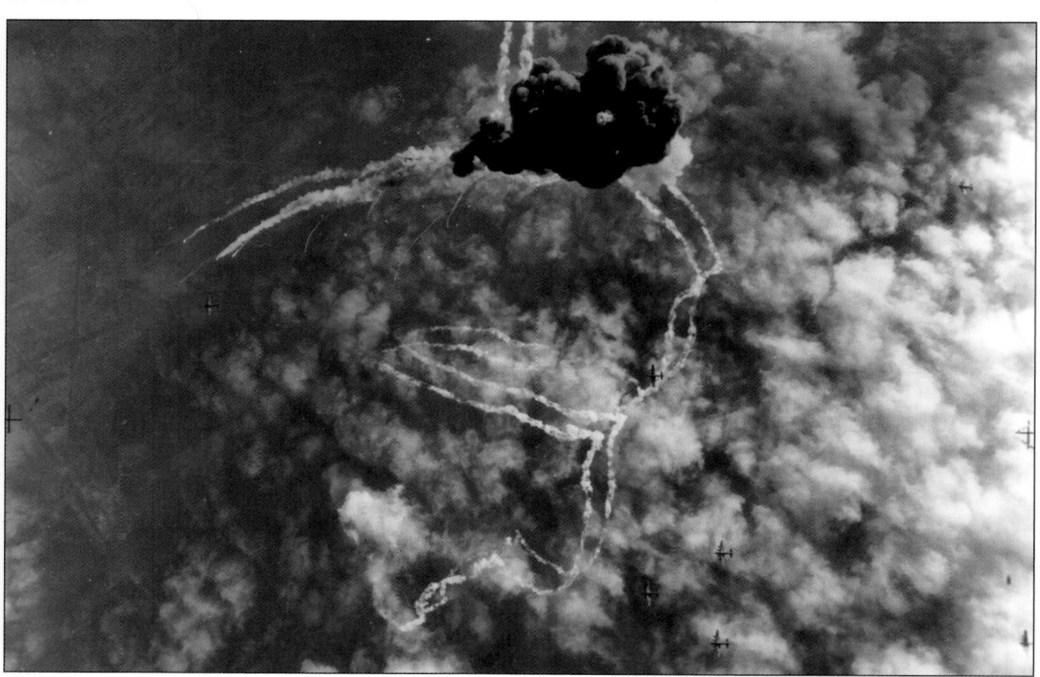

Above Right: Death could come at any time for the young men of Bomber Command. At any moment during their long flights over enemy territory a lurking night fighter or well aimed flak burst could end their lives in a split second. This unimaginable tension was endured by all bomber aircrew, especially when aircraft blew up near them. This photograph, taken on 19th February 1945 is believed to show the explosion of PD336 WP-P and the death of the C/O of 90 Squadron and his crew, Wing Commander P Dunham DFC , Flying Officer Metcalfe, Flying Officer Carlton, Sergeant Page, Sergeant Bozeat, Pilot Officer Creswell and Sergeant Bennet.

Below: Just two weeks earlier on 2nd/3rd February 1945 the same Lancaster PD336 WP-P had been involved in a collision with another 90 Squadron Lancaster HK610 WP-Z. The latter, flown by Wing Commander William Bannister, a pre-war Olympic athlete, crashed with the loss of all on board.

97

(Straits Settlements)

SQUADRON

5 GROUP
8 (PFF) GROUP

Code Letters

OF

Operated the Lancaster from January 1942 - July 1946

Wartime Bases
Coningsby
3/42 Woodhall Spa
4/43 Bourn
4/44 Coningsby

Raids flown with Lancasters
388

Lancasters lost
101 plus 26 in accidents

Points of Interest
Flew the Manchester for nearly a year before converting to the Lancaster. Became one of the busiest Lancaster squadrons in Bomber Command and took part, with 44 Sqn, in the famous Augsburg Raid.

Left and Below: Lancaster PB410 OF-J carries the typical higher visibility markings applied to 5 Group aircraft in summer/ autumn 1944. The code letters are outlined in yellow along with them being repeated on the tailplane.

Below: R5609 is an early Lancaster just like R5482 at the bottom of the page, note the different style of 97 Squadron codes. She is quite different however, note the strangely bulged bomb-bay and radar aerials on the nose, both gained whilst she was with the Telecommunications Flying Unit and the A&AEE.
Note the different sheen between the paint used for the roundel and the extra matt black used on the fuselage.

Below: The burnt out wreck of Lancaster R5548 OF-A at Woodhall Spa on 28th December 1942. The damage to this veteran aircraft was caused by photoflashes accidentally being discharged in the fuselage.

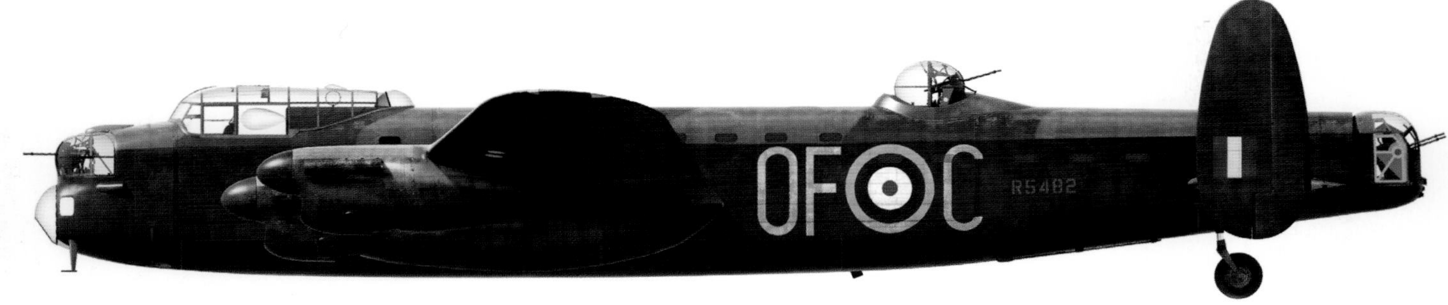

Above: R5482 took part in 97 Squadron's first Lancaster operation and carries unusually thin codes.

100 SQUADRON

1 GROUP

Code Letters

HW

JA and FZ

Operated the Lancaster from Dec 1942 - May 1946

Wartime Bases
Waltham
4/45 Elsham Wolds

Raids flown with Lancasters
280

Lancasters lost
92
plus 21 in accidents

Points of Interest
Before the squadron was reformed on Lancasters, it had been operating obsolete Vildebeests against the Japanese out of Malaya.

Above: 100 Squadron was unusual in having three different squadron codes. EE140 wore the FZ codes when she crash landed at Waltham on 17th June 1943 on her return from Cologne.

Right: This Lancaster 'Winged Victory' was coded JA-U, seen here in 1944.

Below: And wearing the HW codes is ND644 HW-N. A proud member of ground crew, Sgt H. W. Williams shakes hands with Canadian pilot Flt Lt H. G. Topliss as N 'Nan' proudly displays her 112 sorties. The other 'erks' are L-R: AC1 F. Turrell, LAC J. Atkinson and LAC B.Gorst.
Of interest are the exhaust shroud extensions, added by a few squadrons, to further hide the glow from the exhausts.

101
SQUADRON

1 GROUP

Code Letters

SR

Operated the Lancaster from October 1942 - August 1946

Wartime Bases
Holme-on-Spalding Moor
6/43 Ludford Magna

Raids flown with Lancasters
308

Lancasters lost
113
plus 33 in accidents

Points of Interest
The squadron was the only Lancaster unit in Bomber Command to be fitted with ABC, (Airborne Cigar). As such it was required to fly more missions than any other Lancaster squadron in 1 Group.

Right: DV302 SR-H was a veteran Lanc which flew 121 operational sorties, all with 101 Squadron. This photo nicely shows the shape and size of the ABC aerials.

Right: Winter 1943 and the crew of DV267 SR-K climb aboard ready for a long and cold night ahead. note there are eight crew members, the extra one being the special operator for the ABC equipment.

Above: DV245 SR-S 'The Saint' was another centurion Lanc on the squadron. Unfortunately, unlike DV302, 'The Saint' didn't survive its 121st sortie, shot down over Bremen by an Me262. Note the Rose rear turret.

Left: An ABC equipped Lancaster about to receive her quota of oil. The nose ABC aerial is clearly visible, note that it is fitted on the starboard side of the nose, the fuselage aerials were offset to port.

Below: ED382 SR-J was named after 'Joe' Stalin. The 'Joe' was painted in white and the code letters on the port side were SR-J and not J-SR as appears in other publications.

AIRBORNE CIGAR A.B.C.

It was realised fairly early on in the Second World War how important ground control was to an organised air defence system. Consequently it soon became apparent that disrupting this control could radically cut the effectiveness of a defending fighter force.
In summer 1943, RAF Bomber Command had been experimenting with this concept by transmitting interference either against the Freya radar signals codenamed 'Mandrel' or on an even simpler basis, finding the enemy controller's wavelength and blasting it with the noise from a microphone placed inches inside a Lancaster's engine nacelle! (Codenamed Tinsel).
By October 1943, these concepts had been refined into a system known as A.B.C. (Airborne Cigar).
This new countermeasure involved a German speaking eighth crew member flying in a specially equipped Lancaster, listening out for German fighter controller's voice transmissions. As soon as he located a signal, he turned on a powerful transmitter, tuned it in to the frequency and then flooded it with interference. The 'Special Operator' and his equipment was positioned half way down the fuselage between the main spar and the mid upper turret.
101 Squadron was chosen to be the only Lancaster unit to operate this system which they did with distinction for the rest of the war. Its ABC equipped Lancs could be distinguished externally by three 7 ft aerials being attached to the airframe, (one under the nose and two on the upper fuselage). Being the only Lancaster unit so equipped meant that 101 was called upon for almost every operation, large or small. Consequently it flew more operations than most other squadrons and also suffered more losses, especially as any signal transmitted by a bomber could be used by a fighter to locate it.

Left: A still from an official film showing NG126 SR-B releasing her incendiaries on a daylight raid over Duisburg on 14th October 1944, the beginning of Operation Hurricane. This operation set out to demonstrate the overwhelming Allied air superiority by mounting a concentrated attack by US and RAF bombers in the shortest time period possible. As a result, nearly 9,000 tons of bombs fell on Duisburg in less than 48 hours.

Below: Summer 1945 and PA238 SR-Z thunders down the runway at Pomigliano, Italy with her cargo of Allied servicemen heading for home. Because of the wrecked transport infrastructure between Italy and the UK, Operation Dodge was introduced to employ Lancasters as troop carriers to bring the troops home. The choice of the codeword 'Dodge' was regarded as an oblique and unkind reference to the troops in Italy being referred to as 'D-Day Dodgers', a phrase coined by those involved in the D-Day landings.

Note both of these aircraft have the codes 'reversed' to normal positioning, ie B-SR instead of SR-B. This unusual style featured on many of the squadron's aircraft.

SQUADRON

1 GROUP

Code Letters

PM

Operated the Lancaster from
Oct 1942 - Nov 1945

Wartime Base
Elsham Wolds

Raids flown with Lancasters
344

Lancasters lost
135
plus 22 in accidents

Points of Interest
1 Group's busiest squadron, flying the most raids and suffering the highest losses. Life on the squadron was recorded in one of the best books ever written about Bomber Command, 'No Moon Tonight' by Don Charlwood.

Above: On 20th July 1944, several targets were attacked including the V-Weapon site at Wizernes in France. This vertical shot shows PM-E or F high over the target. The amount of bomb craters clearly shows the importance placed upon the V-Weapon targets.

Below: ED724 'PM-M' prepares for take-off from Elsham Wolds on 26th March 1943, her target for the night, Duisburg in Germany.

Left: PM-Y sits at dispersal soaking up the summer sunshine.

Below Left: ED888 'Mike Squared', Bomber Command's top scoring Lancaster, seen here after completing her record breaking 140 ops. Approximately half were flown with 103 Sqn, the other half with 576 Sqn to whom she was transferred when the unit was formed out of 103 Sqn in November 1943.

Bottom: A 103 Squadron crew boards a very clean and new looking ED646 PM-V in March 1943. This aircraft lasted quite a while before failing to return from Berlin on 1st September 1943. Note how the code letters have been painted over the fuselage windows, a common sight on ED series Lancs before they were removed entirely on later series aircraft.

106 SQUADRON

5 GROUP

Code Letters

ZN

Operated the Lancaster from
May 1942 - Feb 1946

Wartime Bases
Coningsby
9/42 Syerston
11/43 Metheringham

Raids flown with Lancasters
370

Lancasters lost
105 plus 18 in accidents

Points of Interest
Guy Gibson commanded 106 immediately before going on to form 617 Sqn.
Sergeant Norman Jackson was awarded the VC for his actions on the night of 26th April 1944.

Above: An interesting photo showing a very large crew (!) walking away from R5573 ZN-B at Syerston in the winter of 1942. Close examination of this photograph shows R5573 to be fitted with a non standard bulged bomb bay. This local modification was introduced to allow 8000lb bombs to be carried long before the standard bulged bomb bays were introduced.

Below: Future Dambusters. Lewis Burpee and his crew photographed on their return from Berlin on 18th January 1943. L-R Sgt Joe Brady, Sgt William Long, Sgt Guy Pegler, Flt Sgt Lewis Burpee, Flt Sgt Eddie Leavesley, Sgt George Goodings. The Lancaster is W4842 ZN-H, destined to be lost over Essen on 28th May of that year, which was just 10 days after the four men on the left had died on the Dams raid.

Above: During the summer of 1944, Bomber Command experienced a shortage of Medium Capacity bombs. As a result, American 500 and 1000lb were used although their box tails proved troublesome to fit in the British bomb bays. These American bombs can be seen here in the foreground in front of 'Here's Home' at Metheringham.

Right: One of the most important preparations for flight was to replenish the oxygen supply. Here, ZN-D is about to receive her quota, note the substantial nose art that she is decorated with!

Below: Metheringham, 1944 and the peace of a March evening is shattered as 106 Squadron taxies out for another night's work. One can almost hear the throbbing of the engines and the squeaking brakes as the Lancasters join the procession for take off.

Members of 106 Squadron group for a photo in front of ED593 ZN-Y 'Admiral Prune II', to mark the completion of the C/O's tour of operations. He was none other than Wg Cdr Guy Gibson, (who was later to lead the famous Dambuster Raid) and ED593 was his regular aircraft. He is standing immediately behind the dog's left shoulder. The Nautical name probably stemmed from Guy Gibson's time on 83 Squadron when he flew Hampdens named Admiral Foo Bang and Admiral Imaz Dryazel, (the latter suggesting the pilot needs urgent refreshment)!

SERGEANT NORMAN CYRIL JACKSON VC

Norman Cyril Jackson originally joined the RAF as an engine fitter before converting to aircrew as a Flight Engineer on Lancasters with 106 Squadron.

On 26th April 1944, Jackson, on his 60th operational sortie, was part of a crew detailed to bomb Schweinfurt. Shortly after leaving the target area, their Lancaster was attacked by a fighter which scored many hits and started a fire in the starboard wing. Slightly wounded by shell splinters, Jackson suggested he climb out onto the wing with an extinguisher and try to douse the flames. With his captain's permission he jettisoned the escape hatch above the pilot's head and crawled back over the cockpit and down towards the burning wing. His progress was hampered by his parachute pack opening and spilling his parachute into the cockpit. The pilot, bomb aimer and navigator took hold of his rigging lines and eased them out with Jackson's progress. Unfortunately the freezing cold and 200mph slipstream made Jackson slip and although he caught hold of an intake on the leading edge, the fire extinguisher was lost and Jackson's badly burnt hands had little strength left. Inevitably Jackson lost his grip and was swept through the fire and was observed to be falling with a partially inflated and burning parachute. The aircraft was abandoned and four of the remaining crew landed safely.

Remarkably Norman Jackson survived his heavy landing but his many injuries saw him spend 10 months in a German hospital as a POW. His citation praised Jackson's ready willingness to face the dangers he set himself, 'providing an example of self-sacrifice which will ever be remembered'.

115 SQUADRON

3 GROUP

Code Letters

KO

and IL (C Flt)

Operated the Lancaster from March 1943 - Jan 1950

Wartime Bases
East Wretham
8/43 Little Snoring
11/43 Witchford

Raids flown with Lancasters
288

Lancasters lost
110
plus 22 in accidents

Points of Interest
The busiest squadron in 3 Group in terms of sorties and losses, 115 also holds the sad record of having the highest number of losses of any squadron in Bomber Command.

Above: 115 Squadron was one of the few squadrons to use the Hercules powered MkII Lancs in any great numbers. Seen here in the summer of 1943 is a freshly delivered DS685 KO-A. Sadly, she didn't last long, on 2nd/3rd August 1943 she and her young crew failed to return from Hamburg, one of 13 Lancasters lost that night.

Below: IL-L of the 'C' Flight returns to an overcast Witchford after a raid on Dortmund on 12th March 1945. Note that this is a Merlin powered variant with bulged bomb doors.

Above: NN754 IL-F of 'C' Flight, another aircraft fitted with the Rose rear turret. The two yellow bars on the fin indicate a Gee-H Leader's aircraft.

Right: This Lancaster II returned from Cologne on 29th June 1943 without her rear turret and gunner. Although some books attribute this to a running fight with two FW190 night fighters, the lack of other damage to the airframe could suggest that a falling bomb was to blame. Note the contours of the bulged bomb bay, fitted as standard to MKIIs.

Left: The crew of HK545 board their Merlin powered Lancaster. This aircraft became another of 115's record losses when she failed to return from Gelsenkirchen on the night of 12th/13th June 1944, shortly after this photograph was taken. Note the clover shaped gas detection patch on the rear fuselage near the rear turret.

138 SQUADRON

3 GROUP

Code Letters

AC and NF

Operated the Lancaster from March 1945 - Sept 1947

Wartime Base
Tuddenham

Raids flown with Lancasters
9

Lancasters lost
1

Points of Interest
Spent most of the war as a Special Duties Squadron. Converted back to normal bomber operations in March 1945, hence the small number of ops recorded.

Above: Although of poor quality this is one of the few photos to show a 138 Squadron Lancaster operational during the war. It is PP675 AC-F complete with bulged bomb bay doors and Gee-H Leader bars on the fins.

Below: In the summer of 1945, many Lancaster squadrons were called to take part in Operation Dodge. This involved the repatriation of Allied servicemen from Italy, many of whom had been away from home for years. 138 Squadron was involved in this operation as can be seen by AC-Z (below) and HK692 AC-Q, (bottom), the graffiti tells its own story!

149 (East India) SQUADRON

3 GROUP

Code Letters

OJ

and TK (C Flt)

Operated the Lancaster from August 1944 - Nov 1949

Wartime Base
Methwold

Raids flown with Lancasters
110

Lancasters lost
4 plus 1 in an accident

Points of Interest
One of only two squadrons who can claim continuous service throughout the war with Bomber Command.
Flew the most Stirling sorties in Bomber Command and had Flt Sgt Middleton receive a posthumous VC on the type in November 1942.

Above: The winter of 1944 was a particularly harsh one, but operations had to continue wherever possible. Here a Gee-H leader taxies around the perimeter track surrounded by a particularly spectacular morning's frost.

Below: 149 lined up with their aircraft at the end of the war. The number of men standing by each aircraft would suggest that this photo was taken during Operation Exodus, the repatriation of POWs from the continent.

Below: NF971 OJ-P sits in the sun at Methwold during the closing months of the war, note the unshrouded exhausts.

Above: 'Chocks away!' PB509 OJ-C a Gee-H leader with horse and chariot nose art starts to roll from her dispersal, early 1945.

Below: Another Gee-H leader, this time HK795 TK-B of 149 Squadron's 'C' Flight. Note the extended section behind the bulged bomb doors and the enlarged astrodome. Although comparatively early in the serial range of Lancasters, HK795 wasn't delivered until February 1945, being one of the last of a batch of 200 Lancasters built at the Castle Bromwich factory.

SQUADRON

1 GROUP

Code Letters

Operated the Lancaster from Nov 1944 - Nov 1945

Wartime Bases

Fiskerton

11/44 Hemswell

Raids flown with Lancasters

73

Lancasters lost

6

plus 2 in accidents

Points of Interest

After operating Wellingtons in the Middle East, 150 was reformed from the 'C' Flight of 550 Squadron at Fiskerton in November 1944.

Right: One for the album. An unknown airman poses with IQ-X at a chilly looking Hemswell in 1945.

Below and profile: Varga style girls were clearly a popular theme with 150 Squadron, NN742 IQ-U sported a similar design to IQ-X.

Bottom: IQ-Y thunders in low over the flooded fields of Holland during an Operation Manna food drop, early May 1945. 'Y' is believed to be JB613 flown by Flt Sgt McAllister. Note the circular gas detection patch on the nose, a precaution that was generally discontinued by all but 1 Group.

153 SQUADRON

I GROUP

Code Letters

P4

Operated the Lancaster from Oct 1944 - Sept 1945

Wartime Bases
Kirmington
10/44 Scampton

Raids flown with Lancasters
75

Lancasters lost
22
plus 4 in accidents

Points of Interest

After being a night fighter squadron in the Middle East for three years, 153 was reformed in October1944 from elements of 166 Squadron.

Right: A crew on their second tour, nearly all Officers!
Door l-r,
P/O Railton-Jones bomb aimer,
F/O Crowley m/u gunner.
Standing l-r,
F/S Arndell wireless op
F/O Bishop navigator
Sqn Ldr Day pilot
P/O Saker flight engineer
F/O Whitewood rear gunner

The aircraft is RA545 P4-X which completed 14 ops with the squadron in the last few months of the war.

Above: Flying Officer Jack Heaton and his crew on top of PA168 P4-G 'George'. This crew was very involved with Operation Manna, flying five sorties in nine days dropping food to the Dutch civilians.
Of interest for modellers is the position and size of the whip aerials.

L-R fuselage:
Jack Heaton, pilot
Alun Evans, flight engineer
Bill Edmonds, navigator
John Gist, rear gunner
L-R front:
Paddy Cossett, m/u gunner
Taff Owen, wireless op
Norman Kirkman, bomb aimer

A formal shot of 'B' Flight 153 Squadron in front of one of its Lancasters at Scampton in early 1945

156 SQUADRON

8 (PFF) GROUP

Code Letters

GT

Operated the Lancaster from Jan 1943 - Sept 1945

Wartime Bases
Warboys
3/44 Upwood

Raids flown with Lancasters
230

Lancasters lost
104
plus 16 in accidents

Points of Interest

An original Pathfinder squadron, it suffered the most Lancaster losses in the PFF force and lost four C/Os in the four months from January-April 1944.

Above: ND875 GT-Q carries a very distinctive aerial above the rear turret. This was part of the 'Boozer' rearward facing radar system which detected radar signals being beamed at the aircraft. This helped to warn the crew that they were being tracked by an enemy fighter, although in practice it picked up various other signals and produced too many false alarms.

Left: Towards the end of the war, many 156 Squadron Lancs appear to have had their spinners painted, GT-Z here having red whilst blue has also been noted on other aircraft.

Below: Believed to be a 156 Squadron crew, this angle shows nicely the mass balances on the elevator trim tabs.

166 SQUADRON

1 GROUP

Code Letters

AS

Operated the Lancaster from Sept 1943 - Nov 1945

Wartime Base
Kirmington

Raids flown with Lancasters
215

Lancasters lost
114 plus 19 in accidents

Points of Interest
Formed from elements of 142 and 150 Squadrons on Wellingtons in January 1943, it in turn helped create a squadron when 27 crews were chosen to form 153 Squadron in October 1944.

Above: Flying Officer Wilson brought JB142 AS-P back from Nuremburg on the 31st March 1944 after a night fighter had set the aircraft on fire. The fire must have been dramatic as the mid-upper gunner bailed out! Note the Monica aerial under the rear turret

Below: The aircrew and ground-crew of ME746 AS-R^2 award an honorary DSO to their Lanc after her 100th sortie on 11th March 1945. The oversized medal is being held by Harold Musselmann DFC and Corporal Dennis Terry.

170 SQUADRON

1 GROUP

Code Letters

TC

Operated the Lancaster from Oct 1944 - Nov 1945

Wartime Bases
Kelstern
10/44 Dunholme Lodge
12/44 Hemswell

Raids flown with Lancasters
63

Lancasters lost
13
plus 1 in an accident

Points of Interest
An Army Co-operation squadron on Mustangs earlier in the war, 170 was reformed on Lancasters in October 1944 from the 'C' Flight of 625 Sqn.

Left: 166 Squadron chose to paint its fins yellow for daylight identification markings, as seen here on ME499 AS-D in early 1945. Her wingtips were also painted yellow.

Above: LM732 TC-C seen over the English countryside in early 1945. Of interest is the gas detection patch on the nose and the Rose rear turret fitted with two 0.5 inch Browning machine guns.

Right: The ever present gas detection patch, this time on the nose of TC-E 'Olivia', possibly ND863. The angular shape under the nose is the Window dispersal box. Close examination of the print appears to show a censored Rebecca aerial, the patch over the bomb-aimer's window could also be by the same hand!

186 SQUADRON

3 GROUP

Code Letters

XY

and AP (C Flt)

Operated the Lancaster from Oct 1944 - July 1945

Wartime Bases
Tuddenham
12/44 Stradishall

Raids flown with Lancasters
98

Lancasters lost
8
plus 4 in accidents

Points of Interest
A fighter-bomber unit earlier in the war on Hurricanes, Typhoons and Spitfires, 186 was reformed from the 'C' Flight of 90 Squadron at Tuddenham.

Above: In March 1945, Wing Commander F.L. 'Curly' Hancock took over command of 186 Sqn. He's seen here in June 1945 with members of his crew. Left to Right: Ken Upton (bomb aimer), 'Dickie' Bird (flight engineer), William Walker (rear gunner), 'Curly' Hancock (pilot), Clem Abrahams (wireless operator) and Johnnie Bellion (mid-upper gunner).

Above: A close up the nose art on their Lancaster named 'The Commando' with an impressive tally of 70 missions and three fighters to her name.

Right: Further down the fuselage and 'Dickie' Bird has taken flight leaving four of the crew to give us an idea of the identity of the Lanc. By a process of elimination, XY-C is probably PB139. Note the clover leaf gas detection patch forward of the turret.

189 SQUADRON

5 GROUP

Code Letters

CA

Operated the Lancaster from
Oct 1944 - Nov 1945

Wartime Bases
Bardney
11/44 Fulbeck
4/45 Bardney

Raids flown with Lancasters
48

Lancasters lost
16
plus 2 in accidents

Points of Interest
A brief existence for this squadron, only 15 months in 1918/19 and then 13 months at the end of WW2 as a Lancaster squadron.

Above: A 189 Squadron crew pose with their Lancaster probably taken at Bardney in 1945.

Below: Although of poor quality, this is one of the few air to air photos of 189 Squadron Lancasters known to exist. Of interest is the 5 Group habit of repeating the individual aircraft letter on the tail fin and the yellow outlined codes for daylight operations. Note also that the aircraft is not fitted with exhaust dampers, again an indication of it taking part in daylight raids.

195 SQUADRON

3 GROUP

Code Letters

A^4

and JE (C Flt)

Operated the Lancaster from Oct 1944 - August 1945

Wartime Bases
Witchford
11/44 Wratting Common

Raids flown with Lancasters
87

Lancasters lost
14

Points of Interest
Another fighter-bomber squadron on Typhoons, disbanded and reformed as a Lancaster squadron on 1st October 1944 from the 'C' Flight of 115 Squadron at Witchford.

Top: Bomb Aimer Len Nisbet sits on a 4000lb Cookie in front of A^4-P in the mist at Wratting Common.

Above: Seven 195 Sqn Lancs photographed on a daylight raid.

Above: 195 had a very distinctive application of its A^4 codes, perfectly illustrated by this photo of LM744.

Right: The crew of PB837 A^4-T pose for the camera before setting off for Bad Oldesloe on the 24th April 1945, note the yellow G-H leader bars on the fin.

Background photo: NG162 A^4-W 'Willie the Conk' sits on a remote dispersal at Wratting Common, a veteran aircraft with an impressive bombing tally.

207 SQUADRON

5 GROUP

Code Letters

EM

Operated the Lancaster from March 1942 - Aug 1949

Wartime Bases
Bottesford
9/42 Langar
10/43 Spilsby

Raids flown with Lancasters
385

Lancasters lost
131
plus 19 in accidents

Points of Interest
Introduced the Lancaster's predecessor the Manchester to operational service and flew more sorties with it than any other squadron. Suffered the highest percentage losses in 5 Group.

Above: This is a fascinating photo of two 207 Sqn Lancasters, R5509 EM-G and R5570 EM-F. The nearest Lancaster has clearly had a new tail section added, note the difference in camouflage demarcation. The question is, to which part does the R5509 serial number apply! The other interesting point is that R5509 has the early style fuselage roundel whereas R5570 has the later version. Both have the later style fin flashes.

Below: 13th September 1944 and PD217 EM-Z, sits in the hangar waiting for some care and attention. The previous night she had been minding her own business in the bomber stream over Stuttgart when a 57 Squadron Lanc tried to use the same bit of airspace.

Left: John White's crew pose in front of Lancaster EM-W PB293 in August 1944. Back row: Tweddle, Hahn, White and Webb. Front row: Winton, Peek and Wykes.

Below: EM-F R5570 also appeared in an earlier photographic session along with EM-A and EM-C. Note that R5570 was at this time wearing the old style fuselage roundel and fin flashes.

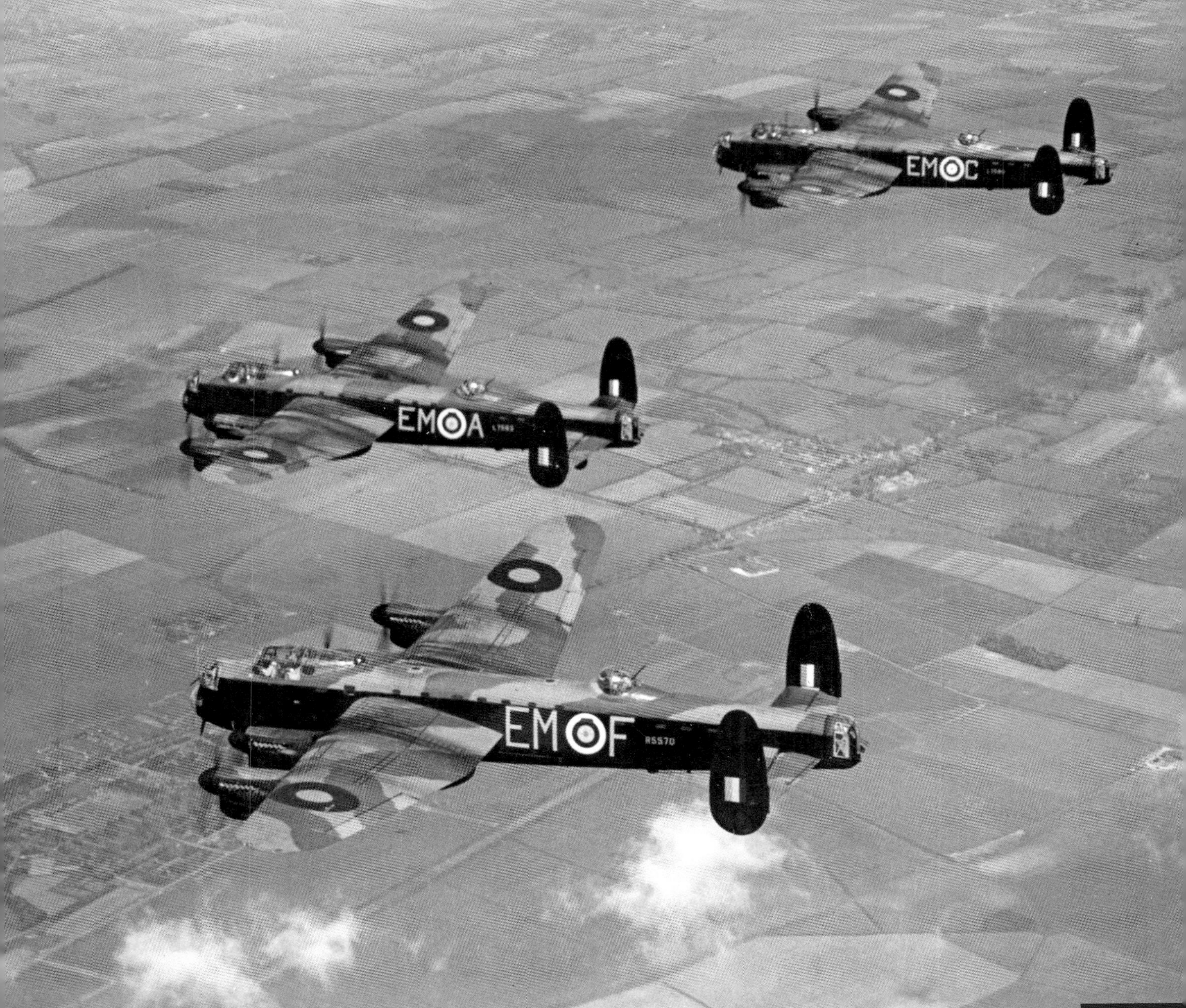

Above: A fine study of an earlier EM-Z LM326 cruising through an autumnal sky in 1943.

Below: L7580 EM-O, one of the first production batch of Lancasters was put on display to thousands in Trafalgar Square in March 1943 during Wings For Victory week.

218

(GOLD COAST)
SQUADRON

3 GROUP

Code Letters

HA

and XH (C Flt)

Operated the Lancaster from Aug 1944 - Aug 1945

Wartime Bases
Methwold
12/44 Chedburgh

Raids flown with Lancasters
127

Lancasters lost
16
plus 3 in accidents

Points of Interest
Suffered heavy losses on Stirlings including Flt Sgt L A Aaron VC before converting to Lancs in August 1944.

Above: 218 Squadron Lancasters taking off from Chedburgh to take part in a 3 Group Gee-H raid on Oberhausen, 4th December 1944. HA-X is NF926, HA-U is PD223. ('X' X-Ray was one of only two Lancasters lost on New Year's Eve on a daylight to Vohwinkel).

Right and Below: 'Bring 'Em Back Alive' HA-B was the regular mount of Flying Officer Ronald Rankine-Wilson.

227 SQUADRON

5 GROUP

Code Letters

9J

Operated the Lancaster from Oct 1944 - Sept 1945

Wartime Bases
Bardney
10/44 Balderton
4/45 Strubby

Raids flown with Lancasters
61

Lancasters lost
15 plus 2 in accidents

Points of Interest
After an existence as a Beaufighter squadron in the Middle East, 227 was reformed from elements of 9 Squadron and 619 Squadron.

The photographs on this page show the C/O Wg Cdr David Balme DSO DFC (above) and his crew together with Lancaster PA280 9J-P on 27th April 1945.
Right: the two gunners, Les Mitchell and Arthur Haywood.

Below: The whole crew, L-R: K Dagnall, Don Brett, Arthur Haywood, Les Mitchell, Johnny Evans, David Balme and Don Richardson.

300 (MASOVIAN) SQUADRON

1 GROUP

Code Letters

BH

Operated the Lancaster from April 1944 - Oct 1946

Wartime Base Faldingworth

Raids flown with Lancasters 138

Lancasters lost 30 plus 6 in accidents

Points of Interest

The only Polish Lancaster squadron in Bomber Command. The unit had soldiered on with the Wellington right up until conversion to Lancasters in April 1944.

Above: SW279 spent a brief period with 626 Squadron before transferring to 300 Squadron in February 1945.

Right: Close up of the nose of Wg Cdr Pozyczka's Lancaster LL804 BH-F probably in late 1944.

Below Air and ground crews line up in front of another BH-F possibly ME470 at the end of the war.

Left: BH-D is probably LM488 which was lost over Kiel on 24th July 1944.

Below Left: A nice close up of a Polish Lancaster just one short of its 50th mission.

Below: Two photos showing a 300 Squadron Lancaster being bombed up. That's quite a weight for the lone erk to be pushing in the bottom photo!

Bottom: A ceremony and service being held at Faldingworth on 1st July 1945.

405 (Vancouver) SQUADRON

8 (PFF) GROUP

Code Letters

LQ

Operated the Lancaster from Aug 1943 - Sept 1945

Wartime Bases
Gransden Lodge,
5/45 Linton-on-Ouse

Raids flown with Lancasters
288

Lancasters lost
50
plus 12 in accidents

Points of Interest
The first Canadian squadron in Bomber Command, 405 was also the only Canadian Pathfinder squadron.

Right: Illustrating the fact that 405 was the only Canadian Pathfinder squadron, the C/O 'Johnny' Fauquier, (centre), welcomes the Pathfinder Group Commander Donald Bennett, (left) to Gransden Lodge.

Below: 405 Squadron in a loose gaggle over a wintry cloudscape.

This page: The Lancaster that Bennett and Fauquier are standing in front of on the previous page is KB700 LQ-Q 'Ruhr Express'. This aircraft was the first Lancaster to be built in Canada and arrived in the UK on 15th September 1943. The photos above and left were part of a sequence taken for publicity purposes to celebrate her arrival. In the photo on the left you can clearly see the twin machine guns mounted in the ventral turret.

Left: In this view of KB700 she has already completed her first two operations. She was then transferred to 419 Squadron where she completed another 46 ops before crash landing on her 49th at Middleton St George.
She was returning from Nuremburg on 2nd January 1945 when she overshot the runway and collided with a mechanical digger. Despite the crew getting out safely, fire took hold and the aircraft was destroyed.

408
(Goose) SQUADRON

6 GROUP

Code Letters

EQ

Operated the Lancaster from Oct 1943 - Sept 1944

Wartime Base
Linton-on Ouse

Raids flown with Lancasters
100

Lancasters lost
41 plus 10 in accidents

Points of Interest
Suffered the highest Lancaster losses in 6 Group and was one of the few squadrons to convert back to Halifaxes from Lancasters, starting in July 1944.

Above: EQ-H sits at dispersal, bomb doors and fuselage door open.

Below: A brand new Lancaster II thunders into the air from Linton-on-Ouse soon after the squadron converted from Halifaxes. The bulged bomb bay doors of the Mk II can clearly be seen as can the abrupt step at the rear of the doors where the seldom fitted ventral turret was designed to be. DS704 didn't see the year out, she went missing over Frankfurt just four days before Christmas 1943.

Above: DS614 with the early style of bulged bomb doors most commonly seen on MkIIs

Right: An anonymous MkII that has had its tail feathers well and truly clipped almost certainly by another aircraft in a ground collision.

Below. A nice line up of 408 Squadron Lancs, presumably for some form of ceremony or inspection?

419 (Moose) SQUADRON

6 GROUP

Code Letters

VR

Operated the Lancaster from March 1944 - Sept 1945

Wartime Base
Middleton St George

Raids flown with Lancasters
127

Lancasters lost
39
plus 14 in accidents

Points of Interest
Flew the most Lancaster bombing raids in 6 Group.
P/O A.C. Mynarski awarded the Victoria Cross for his actions on 12th/13th June 1944.

PILOT OFFICER ANDREW MYNARSKI VC

On 12th June 1944, Andrew Mynarski was a 419 Squadron Lancaster mid upper gunner taking part in a night raid on Cambrai. Without warning, the aircraft was attacked by a night fighter and set on fire. With both port engines out of action, the pilot gave the order to bale out. As Mynarski left his turret he noticed that the rear gunner was trapped, both the hydraulic and manual mechanism having failed. Despite repeated attempts in waist high flames, Mynarski couldn't free the trapped gunner who signalled Mynarski clearly to save himself. Reluctantly, the badly burnt Mynarski left the rear gunner and saluted him before bailing out. His clothing and parachute were by this time well alight and his burning descent was witnessed by French civilians on the ground. Such was the extent of his burns that Mynarski died shortly after he was found.
His heroism would undoubtedly have gone unrecognised had it not been for the remarkable escape of the trapped rear gunner who survived the subsequent crash of the aircraft.

The rear-gunner's testimony made it clear that Mynarski could easily have saved himself but chose instead to try to help his trapped comrade. For this unselfish act of humanity, the brave Polish/Canadian from Manitoba was awarded a posthumous Victoria Cross.

Below: The last Lancaster delivered from Canada was KB999 'Malton Mike' which served with 419 Squadron. It was named in honour of Air Vice Marshal 'Black' Mike McEwen the O/C of 6 Group.

Right: First Lieutenant Joseph H. Hartshorn, an American pilot with 419 Sqn who was awarded an immediate DFC for, in his own words, 'returning from the Ruhr with less airplane than I started out with'. He went on to fly 34 missions and took one of the best Lancaster photos of the war, see below.

Below: First Lieutenant Joe Hartshorn DFC and his crew, William Keelan, Anthony Delaney, Don Lyall, Kenneth Matthews, Frederick Grumbly and Lorne Vince DFM, were responsible for this, one of the most impressive bombing photos of the war. Probably taken on their 23rd op to Falaise on 14th August 1944, the automatic camera fired at the precise moment when Flying Officer Rokeby in KB745, VR-V, drifted underneath them. The 45 degree angle of Rokeby's Lancaster in the photo means that it must have only been in the frame for a split second, making the image even more remarkable.

424

(Tiger) SQUADRON

6 GROUP

Code Letters

QB

Operated the Lancaster from January - October 1945

Wartime Base
Skipton-on-Swale

Raids flown with Lancasters
42

Lancasters lost
5
plus 2 in accidents

Points of Interest
Operated Wellingtons and Halifaxes in the UK and Middle East before converting to Lancs in January 1945

Right and Below: Having only flown Lancs for a few months at the end of the war, there aren't so many photos of QB coded Lancs in existence. Thankfully however, when someone took NG347 QB-P 'Piccadilly Princess' up for an air-test in spring 1945, there was a cameraman alongside to record the scene. Clearly visible in both shots is the H2S blister underneath the rear fuselage. Prominent in the photo below is the repositioned trailing aerial fairing on the fuselage just under the wing leading edge.

426

(Thunderbird) SQUADRON

6 GROUP

Code Letters

OW

Operated the Lancaster from June 1943 - May 1944

Wartime Base
Linton-on-Ouse

Raids flown with Lancasters
53

Lancasters lost
28
plus 7 in accidents

Points of Interest
Operated the MkII only and converted back to the Halifax when MkII production ceased in May 1944.

Left: Members of F/Sgt Stuart's crew inspect DS686 OW-D after their run in with a night-fighter over Leipzig on 20th October 1943. The crew showed great determination in shaking off the fighter and getting home despite being badly hit. The mid-upper gunner Sgt McGovern was wounded. Sadly Stuart and his crew were killed over Frankfurt just two months later in the replacement OW-D LL630.

Left: The ground crew of OW-B admire their nose art featuring a Gremlin pouring a pint for each sortie completed.

Left: DS689 OW-S sits on her dispersal at Linton in the summer of 1943. Before autumn was out she was gone, failing to return from Stuttgart on the night of 7th October.

Below: DS713 OW-J also photographed in the summer of 1943. She lasted just a month longer, failing to return from a raid on Dusseldorf on 3rd/4th November 1943.

427 (Lion) SQUADRON

6 GROUP

Code Letters

ZL

Operated the Lancaster from March 1945 - May 1946

Wartime Base
Leeming

Raids flown with Lancasters
23

Lancasters lost
One in an accident

Points of Interest
Essentially a Halifax squadron that only converted to Lancasters towards the end of the war.

H2S

H2S was a considerable scientific advance for the early 1940s. Quite simply, it was an airborne radar transmitter which scanned the earth below and displayed the return on a small screen in the navigator's compartment. Although it was only at its best when contrasting land and water, this useful ability to identify coastlines, rivers or lakes through solid cloud made a significant difference to Bomber Command's operational capability. The only drawback to the set was that by January 1944, the Germans had developed a device called Naxos which homed in on the H2S transmissions when fitted in a night fighter. They also had ground based sets that could monitor the course of the bomber stream by picking up the H2S transmissions.

Top: This rare view of an unpainted H2S blister shows the scanning dish fitted beneath the fuselage.
Above: The H2S set as fitted to the navigator's table.

Below: ME510 ZL-T was one of only 24 Lancasters used by this mainly Halifax equipped squadron during the war. The H2S blister is only painted at the front to allow the downward id lights to show.

Below: It was very common on bases throughout Bomber Command for a group of well-wishers to assemble at the end of the runway to see the boys off. The constant uncertainty of who would come back combined with the fading light and roar of the four Merlins at full power left a deep impression on most who experienced this ritual.

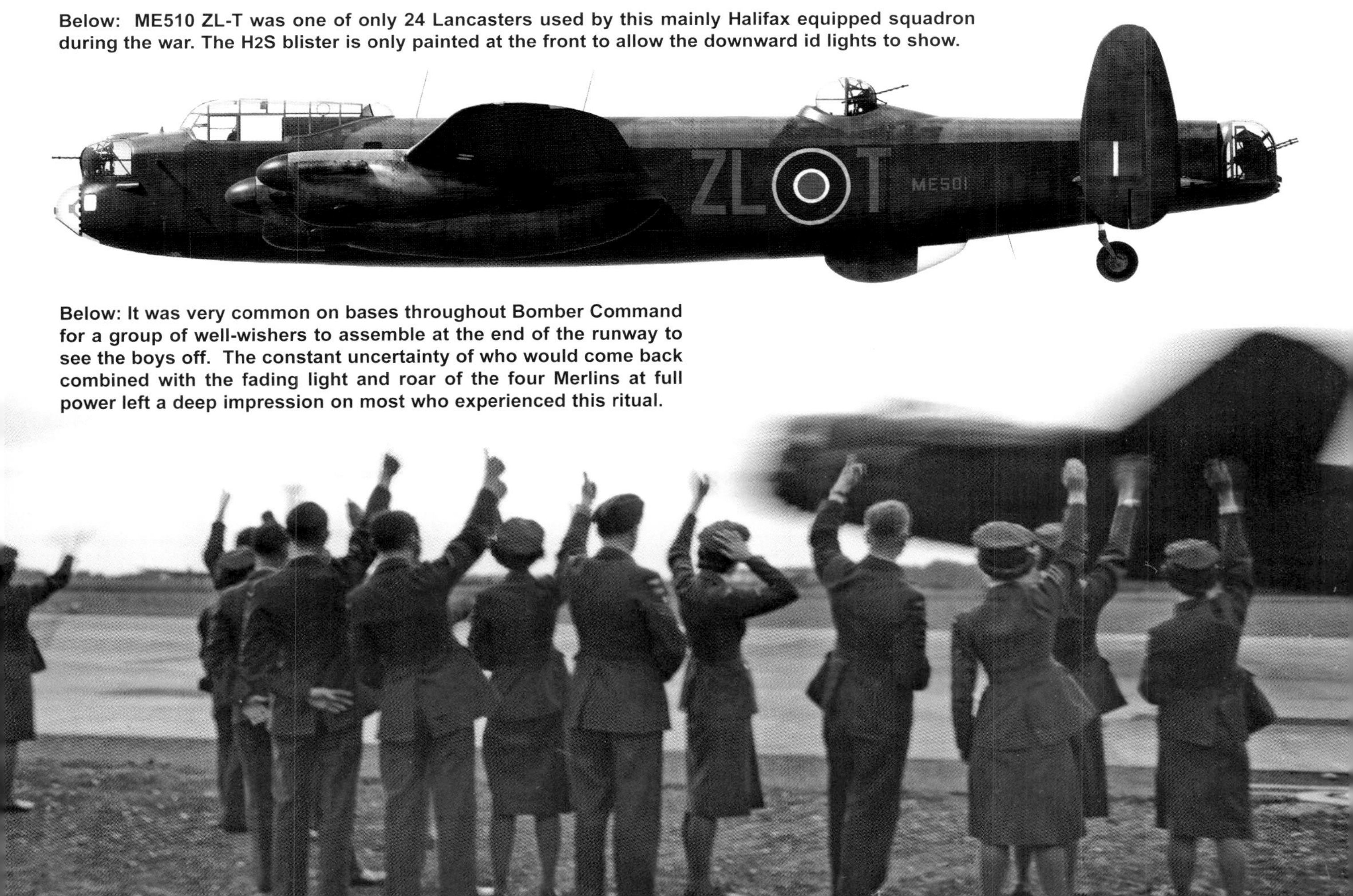

428

(Ghost) SQUADRON

6 GROUP

Code Letters

NA

Operated the Lancaster from June 1944 - Sept 1945

Wartime Base
Middleton St George

Raids flown with Lancasters
111

Lancasters lost
18
plus 10 in accidents

Points of Interest
Another ex Halifax squadron as with most of the Canadian units, had a very low percentage loss rate of only 1.1 percent on Lancasters.

Above: What an emotional moment this must have been. With the war over, the young Canadians head home. Of interest for the modellers is the fact that the two Lancs carry different styles of upper wing roundels, the white ring being reintroduced right at the end of the war. Also note that NA-F has a Martin mid-upper turret, compare its position with that fitted to the Lancaster behind it.

Below and below right: Back home at last! The crew of KB760 NA-P line up to meet the press in Canada. This veteran Lanc of 72 missions was liberally covered in various bits of artwork including apparently, a poem on the bomb doors!

Above Right: Lancaster KB725 rolls off the production line in Canada, ready for delivery to England, note the mid-upper turret hasn't been fitted yet.
Above: The shattered remains of the same aircraft now coded NA-L after she crashed at Elton Hall, County Durham on 3rd February 1945

429 (BISON) SQUADRON

6 GROUP

Code Letters

AL

Operated the Lancaster from March 1945 - May 1946

Wartime Base
Leeming

Raids flown with Lancasters
13

Lancasters lost
1

Points of Interest
Operated Wellingtons and Halifaxes extensively until converting to Lancasters for the last few months of the war.

Above: The threat posed by flak and fighters was still very real, even in the closing months of the war. Here, PA226, AL-H sits at Leeming in 1945 after having her starboard wing ventilated by an Me262 over Hamburg on a daylight raid Close examination of her fuselage reveals evidence of her previous service with 434 Squadron, when she was coded WL-X.

Right: A painting by the author showing PA226 having just been hit by the Messerschmitt 262 jet fighter.

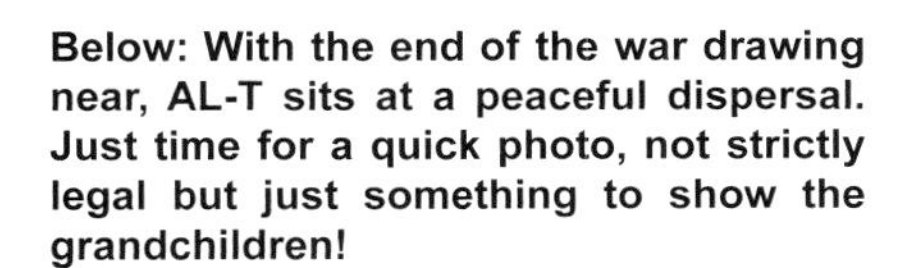

Below: With the end of the war drawing near, AL-T sits at a peaceful dispersal. Just time for a quick photo, not strictly legal but just something to show the grandchildren!

431
(Iroquois) SQUADRON

6 GROUP

Code Letters

SE

Operated the Lancaster from Oct 1944 - Sept 1945

Wartime Base
Croft

Raids flown with Lancasters
51

Lancasters lost
11
plus 4 in accidents

Points of Interest
Formed in November 1942 on Wellingtons, operated Halifaxes for most of the war and suffered the highest percentage losses in 6 Group.

Below: KB837 SE-X had a very impressive piece of nose-art depicting a devil on a cloud.

Above: SE-B probably KB807 in June 1945 on her way home to Canada.
Left: 431 Squadron had some very impressive nose-art, this is KB773 SE-P 'Pete'.

Below: A delicate operation. Lancaster SE-L receives a new port outer propeller with the aid of a small mobile crane. Such work was hard enough at the best of times, but in the cold winter months on the windswept and bleak dispersals of Lincolnshire and Yorkshire it must have been quite a challenge!

432 (Leaside) SQUADRON

6 GROUP

Code Letters

QO

Operated the Lancaster from Oct 1943 - Feb 1944

Wartime Base
East Moor

Raids flown with Lancasters
16

Lancasters lost
8
plus 3 in accidents

Points of Interest
Flew the Hercules engined MkII Lancaster briefly before converting to Halifaxes.

Left and below: ...And there were none bleaker than East Moor. Here with winter rapidly taking hold, DS832 QO-K receives some attention to her starboard inner. She appears to be named 'Miss Leaside' just under the cockpit.

Above: The crew of DS848 QO-R have a final cigarette before boarding. This aircraft was one of the last MkIIs built, the serial range going up to DS852.

Below: Some dispersals could be over a mile away from the main facilities with little or no shelter from the elements. Here an unidentified 432 Sqn Lanc basks in the low winter sunlight at East Moor.

433 (Porcupine) SQUADRON

6 GROUP

Code Letters

BM

Operated the Lancaster from January - October 1945

Wartime Base
Skipton-on-Swale

Raids flown with Lancasters
42

Lancasters lost
3
plus 1 in an accident

Points of Interest
First flew operationally in January 1944 on Halifaxes, only converting to Lancasters in the final months of the war.

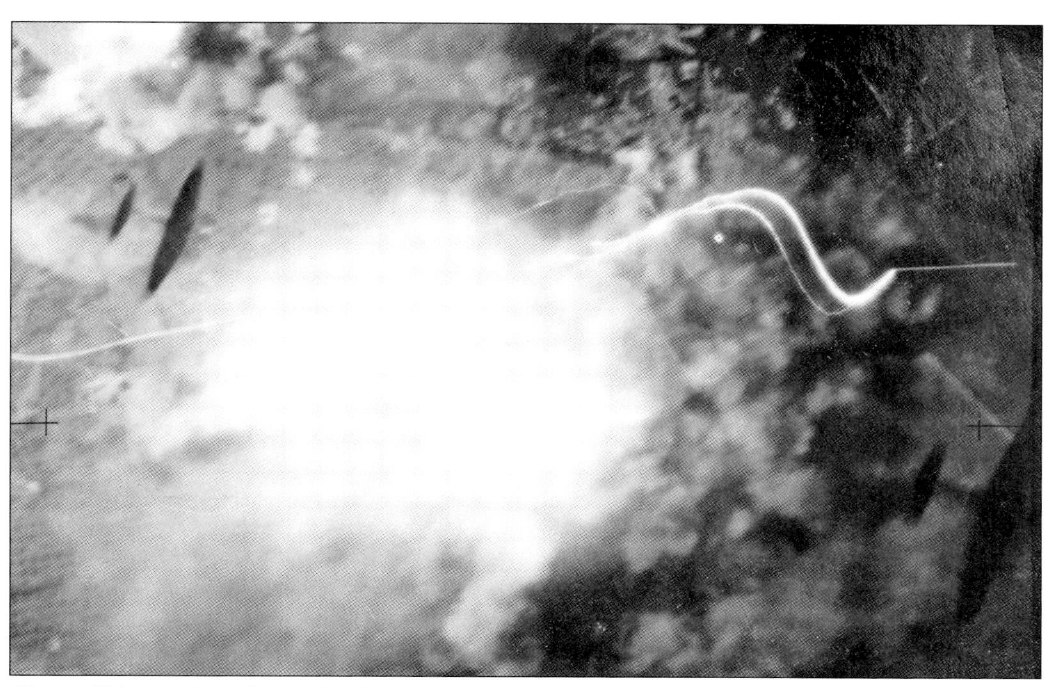

Above: This genuine photo taken by a Lancaster's automatic camera over the target area shows a Junkers 88 night fighter (top left) stalking a Lancaster (bottom right). It has already closed to some 350ft behind the Lancaster, well within range of its nose mounted cannons, and is now dead astern. The outcome of this encounter is not known.

Below: Lancaster R5727 was despatched to Canada in November 1942 to serve as a pattern aircraft for the Canadian built Lancs. The first production MkX was subsequently delivered by the Victory Aircraft Factory to the UK in September 1943. These MkXs soon began to equip all of the Canadian Lancaster squadrons including 433 and did so until the end of the war.

434
(Bluenose) SQUADRON

6 GROUP

Code Letters

WL

Operated the Lancaster from Dec 1944 - Sept 1945

Wartime Base
Croft

Raids flown with Lancasters
41

Lancasters lost
5
plus 2 in accidents

Points of Interest
Another experienced Halifax unit that converted to Lancasters late in the war.

Above: NG497 was one of the few British built MkIs that served with the squadron before being swapped for Canadian built MkXs.

Below: KB883 WL-S 'Hello Sugar' sits with other Canadian squadron Lancasters including KB825 WL-A immediately behind it.

Below: On the 11th March 1945, Bomber Command launched its largest daylight raid of the war by sending 1079 aircraft from all Groups to Essen. Such was the air superiority during those closing months of the war that only three Lancasters were lost on the raid. Unfortunately for 434 Squadron one of these Lancasters was KB834 WL-Y. In the picture, a cloud of Window goes down over Germany as the mass of bombers head for the doomed city.

WINDOW

On the night of 24th July 1943, German radar defences were carefully tracking another big raid heading towards them when suddenly, without warning, their radar screens became a mass of unintelligible plots. The flak and fighter controllers desperately tried to correct their instruments as the hidden force headed deeper into Germany, but to no avail. Hamburg was the target and a force of 728 bombers dropped their bombs on the city virtually unmolested. Only 12 bombers failed to return that night, a mere 1.5% of the total force. By comparison, a similar sized raid exactly a month earlier on Wuppertal had cost 5.4% of the attacking force.

The secret weapon that Bomber Command introduced that night was 'Window', strips of black paper, 27cm x 2cm, with thin aluminium foil stuck to one side. These strips were scattered in their thousands by the bombers and diversionary aircraft to create a blinding mass of radar echoes within which the individual aircraft were completely hidden.

Ironically, 'Window' had been ready for use since April 1942 but had been held back for fear that the Germans would quickly copy the technique and use it in raids on British cities. By mid 1943 however, it was clear that the Luftwaffe was incapable of mounting raids of a similar size and weight and so the device was cleared for operations.

'Window' was routinely dropped from this moment on by Bomber Command aircraft and although the Germans did their best to overcome the difficulties caused by these tiny strips of tinfoil, the invention still stands as probably the most important and influential RCM device of the Second World War.

460

(Australian)

SQUADRON

1 GROUP

Code Letters

UV until May 1943

then AR

Operated the Lancaster from Oct 1942 - Oct 1945

Wartime Bases
Breighton
5/43 Binbrook

Raids flown with Lancasters
307

Lancasters lost
140 plus 31 in accidents

Points of Interest
One of the busiest squadrons in Bomber Command, it flew more Lancaster sorties, (5700), than any other squadron. Consequently suffered the highest Lancaster losses in 1 Group.

Right: ED421 was delivered to the squadron in April 1943 so must have only worn the UV codes briefly. She was lost over Berlin on 23rd/24th August of that year.

Below and bottom: Line up for the press. A group of 460 Sqn personnel line up for the press photographers on a wet and overcast day at Binbrook in 1944. The Lancaster in the background is AR-Q 'Queenie' wearing the customary 1 Group gas detection patch on the nose. This patch was very common earlier in the war but it was mainly 1 Group aircraft that seemed to retain them towards the end of the war. This probably suggests that 1 Group would have been tasked with dropping chemical weapons should the need have arisen at any time. The patch would change colour in the presence of gas presumably to alert the ground crew that one of their weapons was leaking.
The gas patch was also seen in the shape of a clover leaf on some 3 Group aircraft.

Above: 'A' Aussie at Binbrook in 1943. This Lanc ED664 AR-A^2 carried quite a distinctive coat of arms on her nose alongside her bomb tally to proclaim her adopted nationality.

Right: A close up of the nose art of 'A' Aussie with pilot Reg Wellham in the pilot's seat and Flight Engineer Ted Groom sitting on the cockpit roof.

Below: The winter of 1944 was a harsh one with snow falling in many areas. Here at Binbrook the crew and groundcrew of AR-H^2 PB383 pose for a photograph with their Lanc. Note the Boozer aerial above the rear turret and the 'Village Inn' radar hidden under the covers below the rear turret.

463

(Australian) SQUADRON

5 GROUP

Code Letters

JO

Operated the Lancaster from Nov 1943 - Sept 1945

Wartime Base
Waddington

Raids flown with Lancasters
180

Lancasters lost
69
plus 10 in accidents

Points of Interest
Formed from 'C' Flight 467 Squadron and only flew the Lancaster in service. Often flew camera aircraft for the RAF film unit including notably the Tirpitz raids.

463 Squadron had some of the most colourful Lancs in Bomber Command.
Above: A nice close-up of Lancaster 'Cock o' the Walk' with a fascinating array of symbols painted on the nose, reflecting her operational career. It appears that part of the name has been hastily painted over for modesty, possibly before the press arrived!
Below: the crew of JO-X 'Xquisite' sit on the cockpit.
L-R: Flt Lt John Padgham (p), Sgt Ron Gard (rg), Sgt Danny Belton (mug), F/Sgt Don Lewis (nav), F/Sgt Dudley Hannaford (w/op), Sgt Bob Lister (f/e) and in the cockpit is F/Sgt Bert Knight (b/a)

Above: A close up of ME701 JO-F Whoa Bessie's nose art with Flt Lt Bruce Buckham DSO DFC at the controls. Many 463 Squadron Lancasters carried the code and squadron code just behind the bomb aimer's window, a thoughtful touch for future historians!

Below: A peaceful scene of 'Whoa Bessie' at rest on a typically featureless dispersal probably at Waddington. However, the oil stained concrete, the casually strewn gantries and the featureless landscape were common to most airfields, making positive identification sometimes difficult.

Left and Below Left: 463 Squadron also had a Lanc painted with the 'Johnnie Walker' emblem, (see the 9 Sqn page). This one has what appear to be flowers for mission symbols. Note the common 5 Group practice of repeating the aircraft letter on the fin and the yellow outlined codes.

Below Left: JO-Z is RA542 and is pictured here in Sweden after being hit by a Ju88G-6 night fighter over Norway on 26th April 1945. This combat marked the last occasion when a Lancaster was brought down by a night fighter. It is probably symbolic of this terrible war of attrition that the crew of the Ju88 flown by Fw. Gross were killed after being hit by the Lancaster's return fire.
F/O Arthur Cox DSO and his crew were injured but all survived the forced landing just 13 days before the end of the war.

Left: A close up of the nose of ED611 "Uncle Joe" which notched up over 100 sorties with 44 Squadron and 463 Squadron. This photo was taken just as the Lancaster was going off for a refit and general overhaul, hence the 'Goodbye old Faithful' chalked on the bomb-doors.

She returned to the squadron in December and flew another nine ops before crash landing on returning from Pölitz on 9th February 1945 after being hit by a night fighter.

467
(Australian) SQUADRON

5 GROUP

Code Letters

PO

Operated the Lancaster from Nov 1942 - Sept 1945

Wartime Bases
Scampton
11/42 Bottesford
11/43 Waddington

Raids flown with Lancasters
314

Lancasters lost
104
plus 14 in accidents

Points of Interest
The proud operators of one of the world's most famous Lancasters, R5868 PO-S currently residing at the RAF Museum, Hendon.

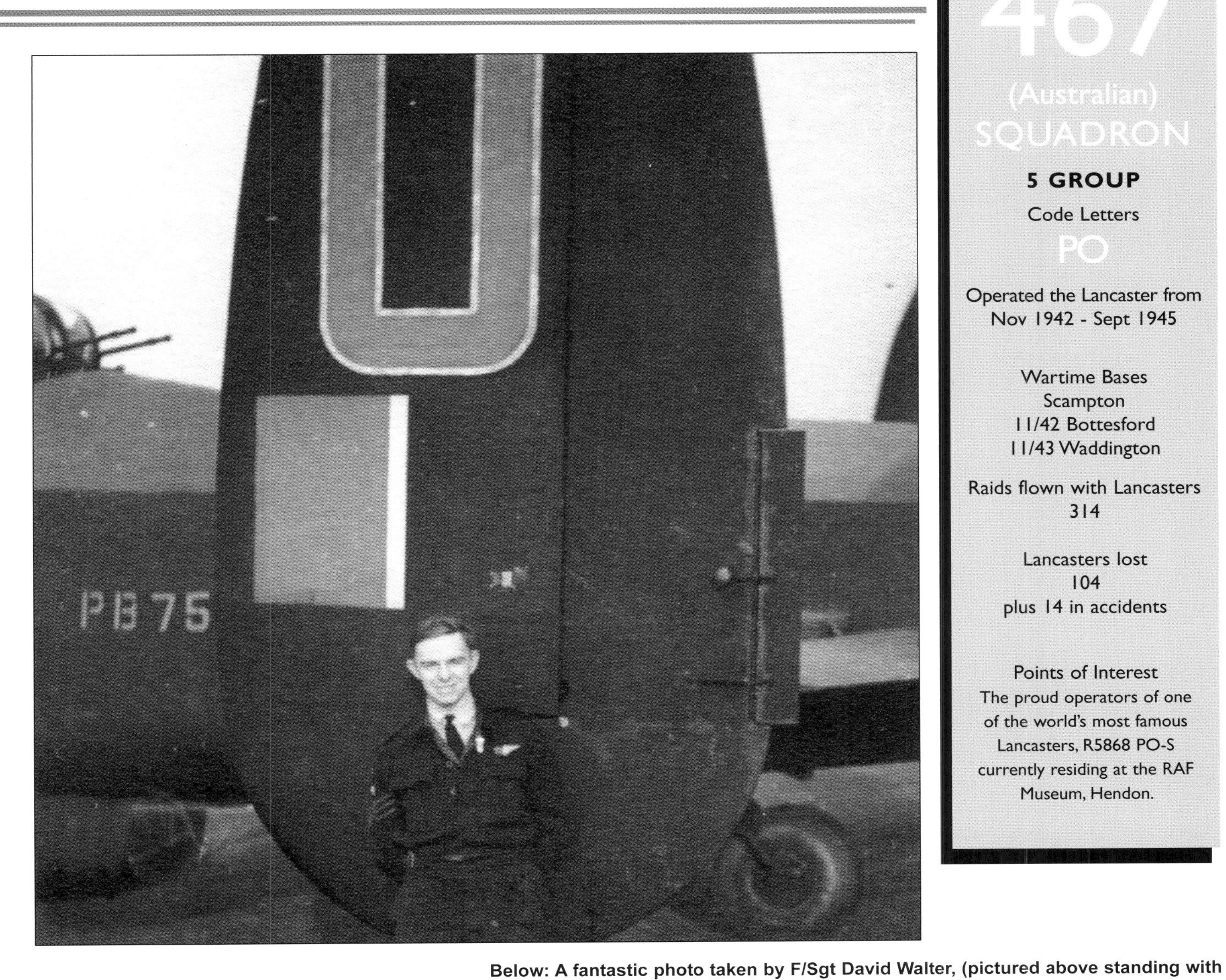

Below: A fantastic photo taken by F/Sgt David Walter, (pictured above standing with PB754 PO-U), of the day when a Lanc crew and a B-17 crew decided to see who could fly on the least amount of engines! In this view all four engines visible are feathered.

Left: Sqn Ldr Keith Thiele's LM310 PO-O limped back from Duisberg on two engines and had to perform an emergency belly landing at Coltishall on 13th May 1943. Thiele was awarded an immediate DSO.

Below: 467 Squadron was one of the many 5 Group units involved in the first Shuttle raid to Friedrichshafen. Here, ED657 PO-Z basks in the North African sun before her return to the UK a few days later. This aircraft was one of 29 Lancasters lost in a costly raid against Duisburg, on 21st/22nd May 1944.

Below: The crew of Lancaster R5868 PO-S line up after flying the aircraft's official 100th mission. L-R F/O Scholefield, F/O Hamilton, F/S Hillas, F/S Hughes, Sgt Burges, F/S Stewart and Sgt Wells. 12th May 1944.

Top: R5868 'S' Sugar, was extensively photographed around the time of its 100th mission. (In actual fact, it may have only been her 91st thanks to some miscalculations by the ground crews!) What is interesting is that on 3rd August 1944, after her '114th mission', she went for an extensive refit and overhaul (middle photos), returning to the squadron in early December. The bottom photo shows her in Germany on 7th May 1945 now displaying 125 missions. In the spirit of a 'spot the difference' competition, see how many changes you can spot!

They include, paddle blade props replacing needle blades, enlarged bomb aimer's blister, 'Z' Equipment rings in blister, Rebecca aerials on nose, new pitot tube, removal of pilot's cockpit blister, H2S blister, just visible, reshaped and yellow outlined codes.

514 SQUADRON

3 GROUP

Code Letters

JI and A2 (C Flight)

Operated the Lancaster from Sept 1943 - Aug 1945

Wartime Bases
Foulsham
11/43 Waterbeach

Raids flown with Lancasters
222

Lancasters lost
66
plus 14 in accidents

Points of Interest
A comparatively short lived squadron, having only ever existed as a Lancaster unit, during the period indicated above.

Below: LL728 A2-L of 'C' Flight which was lost over Kiel on 26th/27th August 1944

Right: RAF Woodbridge in Suffolk was one of three designated emergency airfields designed to welcome any aircraft struggling to reach its home base. These airfields, the other two being Carnaby and Manston, were all situated on the coast and had wide runways and comprehensive repair facilities. In this view taken in the summer of 1944, LL624 JI-P can be seen in the background as fitters work on a Lancaster's starboard outer flap.

Above, Below and opposite page bottom: DS842 JI-F 'Fanny Ferkin II' drops into Deenethorpe, the home of the American 401st Bomb Group in May 1944. Being a Hercules engined MkII, she attracted a lot of attention and was well photographed by the base photographers providing us with nicely detailed images. Note the extra radio aerial under the nose.

550 SQUADRON

1 GROUP

Code Letters

BQ

Operated the Lancaster from
Nov 1943 - Oct 1945

Wartime Bases
Waltham,
1/44 North Killingholme

Raids flown with Lancasters
192

Lancasters lost
59
plus 14 in accidents

Points of Interest
Formed from 'C' Flight 100 Squadron, 550 was another short lived unit that only existed during the period indicated above.

Above and below: Back from Berlin in early 1944 with two dead gunners, DV305 BQ-O displays the scars of her encounter with a night fighter.

Below: ED905 BQ-F receives an enthusiastic send-off as she opens the throttles to depart for her 100th mission on 4th November 1944.

576 SQUADRON

I GROUP

Code Letters

UL

Operated the Lancaster from Nov 1943 - Sept 1945

Wartime Bases
Elsham Wolds
11/44 Fiskerton

Raids flown with Lancasters
191

Lancasters lost
66 plus 9 in accidents

Points of Interest
Formed from 'C' Flight 103 Squadron, 576 was another short lived unit, only existing during the period indicated above.

Above: With her wings yet to be stained by exhaust deposits, a brand new PD235 cruises above the clouds on a training flight in August 1944. Like many of her contemporaries, she didn't have time to become old or loved, becoming a victim of the Calais flak defences on 24th September 1944.

Above and Below: ND521 UL-L[2] looks rather forlorn after suffering a starboard undercarriage collapse on 18th November 1944. She was soon repaired however and continued operations with 57 Squadron. On closer examination there is a small 'saint' figure painted directly under the mid-upper turret.

582

SQUADRON

8 (PFF) GROUP

Code Letters

60

Operated the Lancaster from April 1944 - Sept 1945

Wartime Base
Little Staughton

Raids flown with Lancasters
165

Lancasters lost
28
plus 8 in accidents

Points of Interest
Formed from elements of 7 and 156 Squadrons, 582 was one of the most short lived units in the RAF having existed for a total period of only 17 months. Captain E.E. Swales was awarded the V.C. for his actions on 23/24 February 1945 over Pforzheim.

Above: 60-J and 60-Z heading out on a bombing mission. Note the open radiators on the nearest aircraft, an unusual sight on Lancasters at height.
Below: A 582 Squadron Lancaster on dispersal at Little Staughton. The groundcrew are about to start loading the 1000lb GP bombs lined up in the foreground.

CAPTAIN EDWIN SWALES VC DFC

A SAAF pilot seconded to the RAF with 582 Sqn, Swales was detailed to be Master Bomber for the raid on Pforzheim on the night of 23rd February 1945. Shortly after arriving over the target area, Swales's aircraft was attacked by a night fighter causing considerable damage. Despite this, Swales stayed over the target area and ensured that the Main Force hit the target with great accuracy. Another encounter with a fighter ensued and Swales finally turned for home on two engines with his aircraft losing height. After crossing the Allied lines, the aircraft was becoming increasingly difficult to control and Swales gave the order to bale out. With incredible determination, the brave South African held the plane steady whilst his crew parachuted to safety. Unfortunately he had no time to follow them, the Lancaster plummeted to the ground taking Edwin Swales to his untimely death and a posthumous Victoria Cross.

Right and Bottom: Very rare photos of a 109 Squadron Mosquito and 582 Squadron Lancaster on a daylight bombing run. Both squadrons were based at Little Staughton in the Pathfinder role, using Oboe to mark targets accurately.

Below: Squadron Leader Sooby's bomb load goes down over a V-Weapons site at Mont Candon on 19th July 1944. These bombs are a mixture of 11 x 1000lb and 3 x 500lb bombs. Note the square tails on the front six, indicating American weapons which were used when stocks of British bombs were in short supply during the summer of 1944.

SQUADRON LEADER ROBERT ANTHONY MAURICE PALMER VC DFC

Mention should be made here of the VC award to Robert Palmer of 109 Squadron. A vastly experienced pilot, Palmer had returned to operational flying in January 1944 flying Oboe equipped Mosquitoes. On 23rd December 1944, he was chosen to lead a small daylight raid on the marshalling yards at Cologne. Forsaking his usual aircraft, Palmer elected to take an Oboe equipped 582 Sqn Lancaster and crew. Approaching the target, the formation came under heavy attack from both flak and fighters. Aware that the accuracy of his Oboe guided bombing run would influence the accuracy of the whole raid, Palmer held his aircraft straight and level despite being repeatedly hit. With two engines on fire the crew managed to release their bombs on target, but at a terrible cost, their Lancaster was last seen spiralling down in flames with only the rear gunner managing to escape by parachute. It was Robert Palmer's 110th operational sortie.

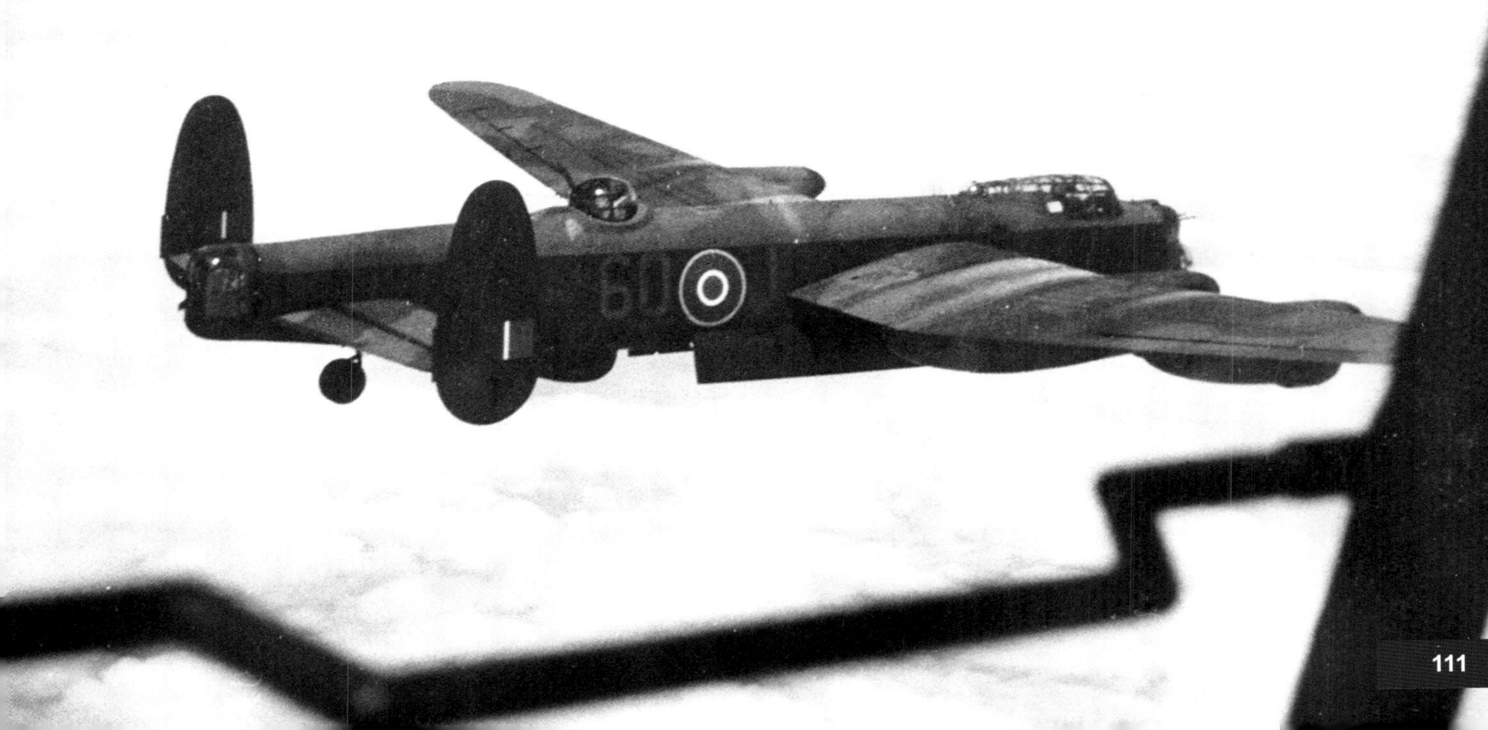

617 SQUADRON

5 GROUP

Code Letters

AJ, KC, YZ

Operated the Lancaster from March 1943 - Sept 1946

Wartime Bases
Scampton
8/43 Coningsby
1/44 Woodhall Spa

Raids flown with Lancasters
100

Lancasters lost
32 plus 12 in accidents

Points of Interest
One of the most famous squadrons of the RAF mainly due to its audacious 'Dambuster' raid of May 1943. Continued on precision raids for the rest of the war and had two VC recipients, Wg Cdr G.P. Gibson and Wg Cdr G.L. Cheshire.

WING COMMANDER GUY GIBSON VC DSO* DFC*

After two tours on bombers and one tour on night fighters, Guy Gibson was chosen to form a special squadron for a special operation. Thus 617 Squadron was born and on the night of 16th/17th May 1943 the 'Dambusters' earned their name by successfully breaching both the Mohne and Eder Dams.

The cost of the raid was high with 8 Lancasters failing to return. Gibson's VC citation suggests that losses could have been higher had it not been for the courage shown by the leader in repeatedly flying low over the target area in an attempt to draw fire from other Lancasters engaged in their bombing runs. In August, Gibson was officially taken off operations and left the Squadron. A series of public and press engagements followed including a high profile tour to the USA, but his yearning to return to operations finally got him back in the air on 19th September 1944, in a Mosquito of 627 Squadron. After completing their duties as Master Bomber over the target area, Gibson and his navigator, Squadron Leader James Warwick, were heading for home when their aircraft was shot down in a tragic accident by a Lancaster's gunners, who mistook his Mosquito for a Ju88 near Steenbergen in Holland, both were killed instantly. This legendary pilot went to his grave with 177 ops and three air to air victories in his log book, he was just 26 years old.

Before he died, Gibson was asked to write about his experiences in Bomber Command. His book 'Enemy Coast Ahead', written with no end to the war in sight, stands as a unique insight into the spirit and determination of all Bomber Command aircrew at that time. It is rightly hailed as a classic of aviation literature.

Left and below: Two of the Type 464 Lancasters that were specially modified to carry the Upkeep mine, better known as the 'bouncing bomb'. ED825 (left) was flown on the raid by Flt Lt Joe McCarthy's crew whereas ED817 (below) didn't take part in the raid but was the only aircraft to drop a live Upkeep in the training flights leading up to the raid.

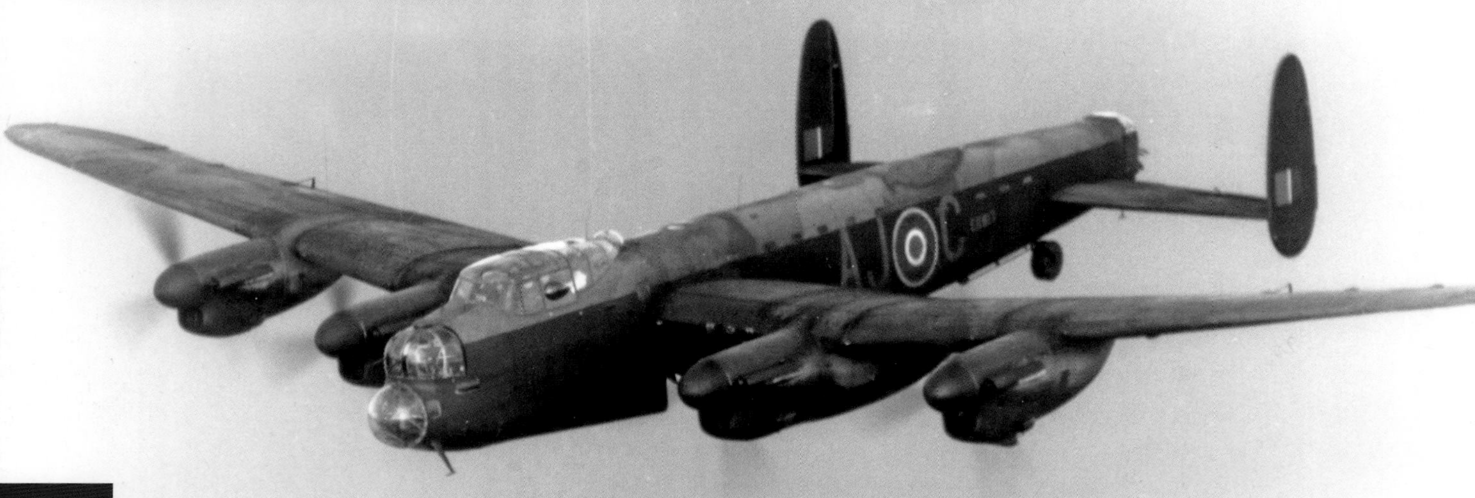

Right: New Zealander Les Munro's faithful Lancaster LM482 KC-W. The nose art is believed to be a witch on a broomstick with a bomb in her hand.

Right: A close up of Bob Knights' Lancaster DV385 KC-A 'Thumper III' nose art, inspired by the character from the film Bambi which had been released in 1942.

Bottom: Both aircraft in formation believed to be heading for Le Havre on 14th June 1944. Both aircraft have bulged bomb doors retro-fitted to enable them to carry the Tallboy bomb.

After the sinking of the Tirpitz on 12th November 1944 the press came to photograph some of the crews that took part. Above is F/O Sanders and his crew with ME562 KC-K. Below is Pilot Ian S Ross and his crew, Nav Terry O'Brien, B/A Ted Tilby, W/Op Ray Ellwood, RG Alec McKellar and F/Eng F Sgt Fryer. Sadly four of these men including Ross were killed exactly 2 months later on the Bergen raid.

GROUP CAPTAIN LEONARD CHESHIRE VC OM DSO** DFC

Leonard Cheshire's VC award is unusual in that it was not given in relation to one specific act of heroism. This exceptional man had already completed 3 operational tours by September 1943 when he took a drop in rank so that he could return to operations as the Commanding Officer of 617 Sqn. With the Squadron, Cheshire developed specialised low-level marking techniques including one night over Munich in April 1944 when, under sustained AA fire, he dived and marked the target from 700ft! Always leading from the front, Cheshire was finally taken off operations after completing his 100th mission.
The award of a well deserved V.C. was for the continuous bravery and inspirational leadership that he had demonstrated during his 4 years of operational flying.

In the closing months of the war, 617 Squadron became the first and only unit to drop the 22,000lb Grand Slam bomb in action. This huge bomb required a specialy modified Lancaster to carry it in the form of the B1 Special. Two of these aircraft PD114 YZ-B and PD119 YZ-J are seen here in formation with a standard Lanc NG494 KC-B.

619 SQUADRON

5 GROUP

Code Letters

PG

Operated the Lancaster from April 1943 - July 1945

Wartime Bases
Woodhall Spa
1/44 Coningsby
4/44 Dunholme Lodge
9/44 Strubby

Raids flown with Lancasters
240

Lancasters lost
77
plus 12 in accidents

Points of Interest
First formed, as a Lancaster squadron, from a nucleus of crews provided by 97 Squadron. Short lived existence came to an end in July 1945 and has not re-appeared since.

Left: Electrical ground crew pose with PG-N 'The Weasel' at Strubby.

Below: LM446 PG-H cruises over a wintry cloudscape in early 1944. She was destined to be one of the five Lancs lost over Genneviliers on 9th/10th May of that year.

Background photo: On 14th February 1944, Main Force had been off operations for over two weeks after the epic and traumatic 'Battle of Berlin'. Members of the press visited 619 on this day and took a series of photos, including this one of LM418 flying through layers of stratus cloud, which provided the press photographer with beautifully balanced light. Points of interest are the extra nose aerial and the reflection of the camera aircraft, (another Lancaster), in the bomb aimer's blister. Note the lack of fuselage windows on this aircraft delivered at the end of 1943.

Left: The crew of 'Pistol Packin' Rosita' LM420 PG-R line up for the camera. Back row: Waterstone, Aitken, Warner, Lowen. Front: Myers, Dack, McNulty. May 1944.

Below: PB842 PG-Y displays the squadron's version of the daylight fin markings introduced in summer 1944. This aircraft was still wearing these colours when she force landed in Sweden on 13th January 1945 following the raid on Pölitz.

Above: A 619 Squadron Lanc is illuminated whilst preparing for take off at Coningsby in 1944.

622
SQUADRON

3 GROUP

Code Letters

GI

Operated the Lancaster from
Dec 1943 - Aug 1945

Wartime Base
Mildenhall

Raids flown with Lancasters
227

Lancasters lost
44
plus 3 in accidents

Points of Interest
Formed from 'C' Flight 15 Squadron in August 1943 on Stirlings, converted to Lancasters in December of the same year.

Below: HK615 GI-Z was one of well over 100 Lancasters that served with 622 Squadron during WWII. She was one of the lucky ones and survived the war, nearly half didn't.

Above: On 16th November 1944, Bomber Command was asked to bomb 3 towns to aid the American advance towards the Rhine. 182 Lancasters of 3 Group were sent to Heinsburg including GI-A, captured here in a bombing photo.

Below: 622 Squadron crews give the thumbs up to a crew already taxiing for take off at Mildenhall. Note the shallow bomb-aimer's blister of the nearest aircraft, an unusual feature in 1944.

625 SQUADRON

1 GROUP

Code Letters
CF

Operated the Lancaster from Oct 1943 - Oct 1945

Wartime Bases
Kelstern
4/45 Scampton

Raids flown with Lancasters
193

Lancasters lost
66
plus 8 in accidents

Points of Interest
Formed from 'C' Flight 100 Squadron and operated Lancasters exclusively for its 2 year existence.

Below: Shortly after being formed, 625 Squadron joined the rest of Bomber Command in the all out assault on Berlin. Night after night the crews made the long and perilous journey to the 'Big City' in the ever worsening winter weather conditions. Here, LM384 CF-X prepares to depart for the Berlin on 16th December 1943. She survived the Berlin campaign only to be lost shortly afterwards over Leipzig on 20th February 1944.

Below: An unidentified crew pose with PB736 at a chilly looking Kelstern, winter 1944/45. The fur lined boots being extremely useful on days like these.

626
SQUADRON

1 GROUP

Code Letters

UM

Operated the Lancaster from Nov 1943 - Oct 1945

Wartime Base
Wickenby

Raids flown with Lancasters
205

Lancasters lost
49
plus 11 in accidents

Points of Interest

Formed in November 1943 from 'C' Flight 12 Squadron and was another unit to only operate the Lancaster during its short lived existence.

Above: The crew of LL849 UM-B^2 made a precautionary landing at Seething after being struck by lightning on the infamous Nuremburg raid of 31st March 1944.

Below: Reg Wellham and his crew look surprisingly happy before embarking on their 25th op, another long haul to Berlin, on 27th January 1944. Left to right are: Johnny Egan (MU), Johnny Atherton (RG), Noel Knight (Nav), Reg Welham (P), Percy Moore (WO), Bill Lamb (BA) and Ted Groom (FE). The Lanc is LM393 UM-W^2, lost 2 months later on 24th/25th March 1944 over the Big City with a different crew.

630 SQUADRON

5 GROUP

Code Letters

LE

Operated the Lancaster from Nov 1943 - July 1945

Wartime Base
East Kirkby

Raids flown with Lancasters
202

Lancasters lost
59
plus 11 in accidents

Points of Interest
Formed in November 1943 from 'B' Flight 57 Squadron at East Kirkby. Has only ever existed as a squadron during the period detailed above.

Top Left: Ron Adams sits in his mid-upper turret of LM287 LE-O in August 1944 at East Kirkby. By this time the aircraft had red fins with black rudders (see above) but had not yet had the code letters outlined in yellow.

Above Left and Left: LE-P LL966 'Prune's Pride' wore a horizontal stripe on the fin which is presumed to be black on red but in comparison to the roundel could be several combinations. Note the thin yellow outline to the codes.

Left: Although at first glance the same aircraft, this LE-P is actually PA266, probably photographed in spring 1945 after LL966 was lost in February 1945. Note the different position of the individual aircraft letter 'P'.

635
SQUADRON

8 (PFF) GROUP

Code Letters

F2

Operated the Lancaster from March 1944 - Sept 1945

Wartime Base
Downham Market

Raids flown with Lancasters
189

Lancasters lost
34
plus 7 in accidents

Points of Interest
Formed from elements of 35 and 97 Squadrons in March 1944. Carried out the first operational trials of the Lancaster MkVI in the second half of 1944.
Sqn Ldr I W Bazalgette was awarded the VC for his actions over Trossy-St-Maxim on the 4th August 1944.

Above: 635 Squadron was given the task of conducting operational trials with the new Lancaster MkVI, pictured here in the form of ND673 F2-V. Note the yellow striped fins and the missing spinners. This photo was taken post-war at a disposal site.

SQUADRON LEADER IAN WILLOUGHBY BAZALGETTE VC DFC

After completing 2 tours of operations, Bazalgette returned to action with 635 Sqn in April 1944. On 4th August of that year, he took Lancaster ND811 to bomb the V1 site at Trossy St Maxim. Shortly before arriving in the target area, Bazalgette's Lancaster was badly hit by flak and set on fire. Despite this he pressed on to the target and dropped his markers. With only one engine still running and the starboard wing a mass of flame the order was given to bale out. Bazalgette however saw that the bomb aimer and mid-upper gunner were incapacitated and so elected to try to put the aircraft down in a field. This he did successfully although tragically, the aircraft then exploded killing all three on board.
It was only when the surviving crew returned to the UK and told the story that Bazalgette was awarded a posthumous V.C.

Below: A fitting final photo for the operational squadron section showing PB935 F2-Z at Lubeck on 11th May 1945 during Operation Exodus. Keen eyes will spot the Meteor jet in the distance, symbolic perhaps of the new era that was dawning across Europe as the ex-POWs were flown home in the aircraft that contributed so much to their liberation.

TOTALS

LANCASTERS BUILT	7377
LANCASTER SORTIES FLOWN	156,192
LANCASTERS LOST ON OPERATIONS	3431
LANCASTERS LOST IN ACCIDENTS	246

TOTAL BOMBER COMMAND AIRCREW KILLED IN WORLD WAR II

55,500

HEAVY CONVERSION UNITS

1651 HCU	1653 HCU	1654 HCU	1656 HCU
Code Letters BS and QQ Wartime Base Woolfox Lodge	Code Letters A3 and H4 Wartime Bases Lindholme Colerne North Luffenham	Code Letters UG and JF Wartime Base Wigsley	Code Letters EK and BL Wartime Base Lindholme

1659 HCU	1660 HCU	1661 HCU	1662 HCU
Code Letters FD and RV Wartime Base Topcliffe	Code Letters TV and YW Wartime Base Swinderby	Code Letters GP and KB Wartime Bases Skellingthorpe Winthorpe	Code Letters KF and PE Wartime Base Blyton

1666 HCU	1667 HCU	1668 HCU	1669 HCU
Code Letters ND and QY Wartime Bases Dalton Wombleton	Code Letters GG and LR Wartime Bases Lindholme Faldingworth Sandtoft	Code Letters J9 and 2K Wartime Bases Balderton Syerston Bottesford	Code Letters 6F and L6 Wartime Base Langar

LANCASTER FINISHING SCHOOLS

No 1 LFS	No 3 LFS	No 5 LFS	No 6 LFS
Code Letters 3C Wartime Bases Lindholme Blyton Faldingworth	Code Letters A5 Wartime Base Feltwell	Code Letters CE and RC Wartime Base Syerston	Code Letters NO CODES USED Wartime Base Ossington

A Lancaster of 1653 HCU lines up for the instantly recognisable runway at Swinderby, note the A46 running parallel to the north-west of the main runway.

The HCUs became the nursing home for many old Lancasters to see out their days, some fared better than others!
Above and inset: R5845 YW-T of 1660 HCU is winched onto a trailer after a heavy belly landing at Winthorpe.
Below: L7532 EK-C was one of the first production batch of Lancasters delivered at the end of 1941 to 44 Squadron. She is seen here at the end of her service life with 1656 HCU.
Bottom: W4154 PE-A was a veteran of the Le Creusot raid amongst others before retiring to 1662 HCU. Note the retro-fitted Rose rear turret and anti-shimmy tail wheel. She then moved on to 1LFS and 1667 HCU where she crashed on landing on 19th January 1945.

POST WAR

Above: SW359 was delivered to the RAF in the summer of 1945 and allocated to 178 Squadron in the Middle East.

With the war in Europe over, RAF Bomber Command was tasked with assembling a force to fly out to join in the war against Japan. 'Tiger Force' was originally to include 30 Lancaster squadrons including 10 Canadian units. Events moved rapidly however and the atomic bombs were dropped before any of the squadrons had been deployed.

Bomber Command was now vastly over-manned and a rapid period of demobilisation started with 26 squadrons being disbanded within the first 6 months of peace. Lancaster production however continued almost unchecked as the plan had been to re-equip the whole of Tiger Force with new Lancasters, specially equipped for FE (Far East) operations.

These new Lancasters with their white/black paint schemes, were fitted with extra navigation aids for the anticipated long hours of operations over featureless oceans. By fortunate coincidence, a lot of Coastal Command's maritime patrol aircraft were being returned to the USA as part of the Lend-Lease agreement, these Lancasters were therefore ideal replacements. Out in the Middle East, some bomber squadrons had also lost their Lend-Lease Liberators and were re-supplied with the new Lancasters. No's 40, 70, 104, 178 and 214 Squadrons were thus re-equipped and provided a show of force in the increasingly tense Suez Canal area.

Back home, a small number of Lancasters had been modified to carry an airborne lifeboat. The ASR III, as it was officially designated, saw service with at least half a dozen different maritime squadrons in the late forties. Other new uses for the Lancaster included a few MkIs being converted into photographic reconnaissance aircraft, these being operated by 541 Squadron, (later reformed into 82 Squadron), and 683 Squadron.

The following RAF units all operated the Lancaster after the Second World War and so do not feature in the main section of this book.

18 Squadron
Maritime Recce, Middle East

37 Sqn, codes LF
Maritime Recce, Middle East

38 Sqn, codes RL
Maritime Recce, Middle East

40 Sqn, codes BL
Heavy Bomber, Middle East

70 Squadron
Heavy Bomber, Middle East

104 Sqn, codes EP
Heavy Bomber, Middle East

120 Sqn, codes BS
Maritime Recce, UK

148 Sqn, codes AU
Heavy Bomber, UK

160 Sqn, codes BS
Maritime Recce, Middle East

178 Squadron
Heavy Bomber, Middle East

179 Sqn, codes OZ
Maritime Recce, UK

203 Sqn, codes CJ
Maritime Recce, UK

210 Sqn, codes OZ
Maritime Recce, UK

214 Sqn, codes QN
Heavy Bomber, Middle East/UK

224 Sqn, codes XB
Maritime Recce, UK

279 Sqn, codes RL
Air Sea Rescue, UK

420 Sqn, codes PT
Canadian Heavy Bomber, re-equipped too late for Lanc ops

425 Sqn, codes KW
Canadian Heavy Bomber, re-equipped too late for Lanc ops

541 Squadron
Photo-Survey, UK

621 Squadron
Maritime Recce, Middle East

683 Squadron
Photo-Survey, Middle East

Above: RF324 RL-K of 279 Squadron on Air Sea Rescue duties fitted with H_2S and an airborne lifeboat, out of Thornaby in 1946.

Above: A Coastal Reconnaissance Lancaster TX268 at dispersal at St Mawgan in 1952.

Below: A close-up of an airborne lifeboat fitted to CJ-F of 203 Squadron.

INDEX OF SQUADRON CODES

2K	1668 HCU
3C	1LFS
6O	582 Squadron
6F	1669 HCU
9J	227 Squadron
A2	514 Squadron
A3	1653 HCU
A3	230 OCU
A4	195 Squadron
A5	3LFS
AA	75 Squadron
AC	138 Squadron
AJ	617 Squadron
AL	429 Squadron
AP	186 Squadron
AR	460 Squadron
AS	166 Squadron
AU	148 Squadron
BH	300 Squadron
BL	1656 HCU
BL	40 Squadron
BM	433 Squadron
BQ	550 Squadron
BS	1651 HCU
BS	120 Squadron
BS	160 Squadron
CA	189 Squadron
CE	5LFS
CE	1668 HCU
CF	625 Squadron
CJ	203 Squadron
DJ	15 Squadron
DX	57 Squadron
EA	49 Squadron
EK	1656 HCU
EM	207 Squadron
EP	104 Squadron
EQ	408 Squadron
F2	635 Squadron
FD	1659 HCU
FZ	100 Squadron
GG	1667 HCU
GI	622 Squadron
GP	1661 HCU
GT	156 Squadron
GZ	12 Squadron
H4	1653 HCU
HA	218 Squadron
HW	100 Squadron
IL	115 Squadron
IQ	150 Squadron
J9	1668 HCU
JA	100 Squadron
JE	195 Squadron
JF	1654 HCU
JI	514 Squadron
JN	75 Squadron
JO	463 Squadron
K7	236 OCU
KB	1661 HCU
KC	617 Squadron
KF	1662 HCU
KM	44 Squadron
KO	115 Squadron
KR	1667 HCU
KW	425 Squadron
L6	1669 HCU
LE	630 Squadron
LF	37 Squadron
LQ	405 Squadron
LS	15 Squadron
M9	1653 HCU
MG	7 Squadron
NA	428 Squadron
ND	1666 HCU
NF	138 Squadron
OF	97 Squadron
OJ	149 Squadron
OL	83 Squadron
OW	426 Squadron
OZ	179 Squadron
OZ	210 Squadron
P4	153 Squadron
PE	1662 HCU
PG	619 Squadron
PH	12 Squadron
PM	103 Squadron
PO	467 Squadron
PT	420 Squadron
QB	424 Squadron
QN	214 Squadron
QO	432 Squadron
QQ	1651 HCU
QR	61 Squadron
QT	57 Squadron
QY	1666 HCU
RC	5LFS
RL	38 Squadron
RL	279 Squadron
RV	1659 HCU
SE	431 Squadron
SN	230 OCU
SR	101 Squadron
TC	170 Squadron
TK	149 Squadron
TL	35 Squadron
TV	1660 HCU
UG	1654 HCU
UL	576 Squadron
UM	626 Squadron
UV	460 Squadron
VN	50 Squadron
VR	419 Squadron
WL	434 Squadron
WP	90 Squadron
WS	9 Squadron
XB	224 Squadron
XH	218 Squadron
XU	7 Squadron
XY	186 Squadron
YW	1660 HCU
YZ	617 Squadron
ZL	427 Squadron
ZN	106 Squadron

A Lancaster returns safely with the aid of FIDO, a fog dispersal system which involved burning streams of piped petrol each side of the runway.